LINGER WITH ME

Moments Aside With Jesus

LINGER WITH ME

Moments Aside With Jesus

Msgr. David E. Rosage

LIVING FLAME PRESS

Cover: Robert Manning

Photo: Craig Callan

All scripture quotations are from the *New American Bible*

Copyright 1979: Msgr. David E. Rosage

Nihil Obstat: Rev. Armand M.Nigro,S.J., *Censor Librorum*
November 25,1978

Imprimatur: Most Rev. Bernard J. Topel, D.D., Ph.D., Bishop
of Spokane, November 25,1978

ISBN: 0-914544-29-2

Published by: Living Flame Press/Box 74/Locust Valley, N Y
11560

Printed in the United States of America

CONTENTS

Preface 10

1. LISTEN TO THE SEED GROWING:
   Praying Is Listening (Mark 4:1-20) 17

2. AND GOD SAW THAT IT WAS VERY GOOD:
   I Love You With A Creative Love
   (Psalm 104) 25

3. WONDER, AWE, REVERENCE:
   Our Majestic God (Sirach 17:1-27) 31

4. MORE THAN MANY SPARROWS:
   The Father Loves You With A Providing Love
   (Mt. 6:25-34) 37

5. WHY DID YOU DO SUCH A THING?
   God Complains About Man's Unfaithfulness
   (Gen. 3:1-24) 43

6. CELEBRATE AND REJOICE:
   Listen To God Say: "I Don't Care What
   You Have Done. I Love You Anyway." (Luke
   15:11-32) 49

7. GABRIEL BREAKS THE GOOD NEWS:
   The Annunciation (Luke 1:26-38) 55

8. GOD RESPONDS TO MAN'S NEED:
   He Made His Dwelling Among Us
   (Luke
   2:1-20) 61

9. BAPTISM OF JESUS:
   Jesus Coming From Galilee, Appeared
   Before John (Mt. 3:11-17) 67

10. TEMPTATION IN THE DESERT:
    Relive With Jesus His Desert Experience
    (Mt. 4:1-11) 73

11. THE BEATITUDES:
    What Was Jesus Like? (Mt. 5:3-12) 79

12. COME FOLLOW ME:
    The Call, Conditioning, And Commitment
    To Discipleship (Luke 9:57-62) 85

13. JESUS MEETS A SAMARITAN WOMAN AT-
    JACOB'S WELL:
    Called To Be An Apostle Of Love
    (John 4:4-42) 91

14. UP A TREE WITH ZACCHAEUS: THE TAX
    COLLECTOR:
    Jesus Knew His Heart (Luke 19:1-10) .. 97

15. BLIND BARTIMAEUS:
    I Want To See (Mark 10:46-52) 103

16. A PARALYTIC:
    Jesus Is Touched By The Faith Of
    The Community (Mark 2:1-12) 109

17. GOOD SHEPHERD:
    Mine Know Me (John 10:1-18) 115

18. THE VINE AND THE BRANCHES:
    My Friend Had A Vineyard (John 15:1-8) 121

19. JESUS FEEDS THE MULTITUDE:
    The Lad Who Shared His Lunch
    (John 6:1-15) 127

20. THE TRANSFIGURATION:
    The Tops Of The Mountains Are His
    (Luke 9:28-36) 133

21. PALM SUNDAY:
    Messianic Entry Into Jerusalem
    (Luke 19:28- 44) 139

22. THE LAST SUPPER:
    I Myself Am The Bread Of Life
    (Luke 22:7-20) 145

23. AGONY IN THE GARDEN:
    Loneliness Too Is Suffering
    (Mt. 26:36-46) 151

24. THE PASSION OF JESUS:
    Test, Temptation, Trial
    (Luke 22:47-71) 157

25. THE DEATH OF JESUS:
   O My People, What Have I Done To You?
   (John 19:17-30) 163
26. APPEARANCES TO THE DISCIPLES:
   "My Lord And My God"
   (John 20:19-29) 169
27. ROAD TO EMMAUS:
   An Awareness Walk (Luke 24:13-35) ... 177
28. JESUS APPEARS IN GALILEE:
   Picnic On The Shore (John 21:1-19) ... 183
29. PENTECOST:
   "All Were Filled With The Holy Spirit"
   (Acts: Ch. 1&2) 191
30. LIVING WITH THE RISEN JESUS:
   "Who Will Separate Us From The Love Of
   Christ?" (Rom. 8:1-39) 199
31. FINDING GOD IN ALL THINGS:
   "When You Seek Me With All Your Heart,
   You Will Find Me With You."
   (John 1:1-18) 207

Preface

In our times God, true to his promise, is certainly visiting his people. Our loving Father is showing us that genuine spiritual renewal will come not from movements and structures alone, but must come from within the hearts of each one of us. He is teaching us also that genuine happiness and peace will come not merely from external innovations, but has its source in the inner renewal of the heart. God promised us through his prophet: "I will give you a new heart and place a new spirit within you, taking from your bodies your stony hearts and giving you natural hearts" (Ezekiel 36:26).

God is doing so by implanting in the hearts of men and women of our age a real hunger and thirst for a deeper, richer, more personal relationship with him. We are experiencing a desire to meet him often in prayer, and are finding ourselves wanting to linger with him for longer periods of time. Prayer is our relationship to our loving Father. It can be expressed in various forms and in many different ways.

PRAYER IS LISTENING

God is calling us to a listening posture in prayer. Within each one of us there is a longing to be alone with him in the solitude of our own heart. There is within us a desire to experience God at the very core of our being. Jesus encourages us in this method of prayer when he bids us: "Come by yourselves to an out-of-the-way place and rest a little" (Mark 6:31).

It is true that many people are attracted to various forms of communal prayer. We enjoy praying with others. Shared prayer has added a whole new dimension to our personal relationships. It does much to form genuine Christian community. Jesus promised us: "If two of you join your voices on earth to pray for anything whatever, it shall be granted you by my Father in heaven. Where two or three are gathered in my name, there am I in their midst" *(Matthew 18:19-20)*. However, these two different forms of prayer are not mutually exclusive. On the contrary, the deeper we enter into the prayer of solitude, the more frequently we meet the Lord in our quiet prayer of listening, the richer will be our sharing and the more we will have to offer when we pray with others.

LISTENING TO HIS WORD

The Lord is leading us into the prayer of solitude as he invites us to listen to his Word as found in Sacred Scripture. We are becoming more and more fascinated and intrigued as we listen to what he has to say to us in the Scriptures. He is drawing us not so much to study the Bible, but rather to listen to his personal message coming to us from his Word. His message is a very personal one and it nourishes us and supplies our needs, especially our needs for that particular day. Praying with Sacred Scripture is not an end in itself. It is a launching pad into orbit with God our loving Father and with Jesus our Lord and Savior. It helps us focus on God, and it enables God to unfold his plans for us.

A FLIGHT-PLAN

This volume is an attempt to delineate a pathway which will lead us into a deeper union with Jesus as well as with the Father and the Holy Spirit. It is not a book to be read at one sitting. It is rather a manual to be used for our quiet, reflective time with Jesus.

This book is a guideline which will steer us on a course covering the whole expanse of our spiritual growth. Before we can begin our journey to a more personal relationship with God, we must be convinced that we are lovable. That is the crux of our spiritual development. So many people have a low self-image. They are not convinced that they are lovable, and they fear not being accepted by others.

Before we can make any progress in spiritual maturity, we need to know that God loves us, and that he loves us just as we are. Listen to him say to you: "You are precious in my eyes and glorious, and because I love you" *(Isaiah 43:4)*. The Father loves us so much that he sent Jesus into the world to restore our union in love with him. "Yes, God so loved the world that he gave his only Son" *(John 3:16)*. Jesus also impresses upon us how much he loves us: "As the Father has loved me, so I have loved you" *(John 15:9)*. It is imperative that we know with our hearts that God loves us so much that he wants us to be united with him for all eternity. Jesus assures us of this union with him when he says: "I am indeed going to prepare a place for you, and then I shall come back to take you with me, that where I am you also may be" *(John 14:3)*. The following pages may be considered a road map to help us plot our spiritual journey. They will help us relive in our own lives the Emmaus experience of Jesus walking with his disciples and opening for them the Scriptures so that they could say: "Were not our hearts burning inside us as he talked to us on the road and explained the Scriptures to us?" *(Luke 24:32)*.

This guideline is intended to be used over a period of thirty or more weeks. Remotely it corresponds to the themes which are presented during a thirty-day retreat. Each chapter offers a theme which is the suggested theme for a week of prayer. There is only one scriptural passage suggested for each week. It has seven subdivisions suggesting a different thought for each day of the week based on the same scriptural text.

This volume is divided into thirty-one chapters. If a person wishes to use one chapter for each day, it forms a convenient prayer-plan for one month. This abbreviated form will be helpful but not nearly as fruitful.

The daily reflection is not an exegetical explanation of the text of Scripture, nor does it suggest the insights which we should expect to enjoy during our prayer time. These brief statements are only hints which may stimulate our thought patterns and draw us into a contemplative posture. The colloquy at the end of our prayer time likewise is only a thought which may help us formulate our own personal colloquy with the Lord.

PRAYER IS LOVING

Contemplative prayer is a prayer of listening and of loving. It is "being for God" and letting "God be for us." It is putting ourselves totally at God's disposal to listen with our whole being. We are not concerned about brilliant thoughts or magnificent insights. We are more concerned about being in God's presence and letting him love us. Jesus encourages us in this: "Live on in my love" (John 15:9).

Contemplative prayer is the prayer of the heart and not of the mind. Meditation is the prayer of the mind. When we meditate we reflect on a truth or a passage of Sacred Scripture and try to draw some conclusions and apply them in our own lives. On the other hand, contemplative prayer is experiencing God's presence, basking in his love and striving to respond to him in love.

PREPARING FOR PRAYER

There are several preparatory steps which will facilitate our entering into a listening prayer. In the first place, we should have a fixed time and place for prayer.

This may be in our favorite chair, our bedroom, a prayer room, or in a chapel. A special place for prayer helps us psychologically for we begin to enter into a spirit of prayer as we approach that spot. As we settle into a comfortable, relaxed position, we can listen more attentively.

Many methods and procedures are suggested for relaxing. Use your own favorite method and relax in the presence of the Lord. Concentrating on breathing is a popular way of letting go of the tensions in our lives. As we inhale and exhale we can mention the name of Jesus repeatedly deep inside ourselves without pronouncing his name with our lips.

Sit, relax and remember that God is present and wishes to speak to you through his Word. Read the text slowly and reflectively permitting every word to find a home in your heart. If a word or expression seems to say something to you, pause and listen. Bask in the sunshine of God's presence. Let his love fill you as you listen.

SPIRITUAL JOURNAL

A valuable aid for deepening our relationship with the Lord is the keeping of a spiritual journal. A journal is a brief record of what happens during our prayer time each day. We cannot judge whether or not our prayer time was good or bad. Only God can know that, but we can record other aspects of our prayer. What thoughts, impressions, experiences, feelings did we have? Was our prayer peaceful and calm, or restless and distracted? Did we have a sense of God's presence? Did we experience his love?

Writing makes us more exact and specific. If we write down our experience in prayer, we deepen that experience. It becomes a part of us and develops into a habitual pattern for our daily living. This writing itself is a prayer. From time to time it is well to read our journal on a retreat or on our day in the desert or at any other time. The rereading of our experience in prayer will enrich and deepen it even more.

FRUITS

Contemplative prayer molds, forms and transforms our attitude, our mentality, our hearts. We may not be aware of the transforming effects of contemplation, but they are taking place nonetheless. As we pray contemplatively, we discover a new zest for living. We find inspiration and motivation for living. The ordinary, routine, commonplace duties and events of daily living take on a new significance. We approach them with a new exuberance. It gives real meaning to all the events of life because it helps us read between the lines.

A second fruit which is often produced in our hearts is a sort of conversion process. We discover that we are becoming less concerned about the mundane, meaningless happenings in the course of each day and are focusing more frequently on the infinite goodness and love of God. We find ourselves speaking our thoughts more freely with our loving Abba. We live with greater freedom and peace. As we listen to God speaking to us we will be singularly blessed. Jesus assures us: "Rather blest are they who hear the word of God and keep it" *(Luke 11:28)*.

Thirdly, as we continue to pray contemplatively by listening to God's Word, a transformation takes place within us. God is forming our hearts. Sometimes he gives us a little glimpse into what is happening in order to encourage us. Frequently he does not. At times we find that we are a little more peaceful, or treating others with greater consideration. We are becoming more loving toward others. We may notice that we now see some good qualities in certain persons who used to bother us. These are only a few ways in which the transformation takes place within us.

All this transpires within us because we have discovered deep in our hearts, once again, that God loves us just as we are. Praying with Sacred Scripture, and listening to what God has to say to us, will make our daily journey through life more delightful and more fruitful. May God bless this attempt to charter such a course.

1 Listen to the Seed Growing

Praying Is Listening
Mark 4:1-20

If you wish to enjoy your favorite television program there are certain preliminary preparations which are required. You must have a comfortable chair in which to sit. You will shut out the excessive noises which interfere with good listening. You would have to turn on your set, adjust it until the picture becomes clear, the colors sharp and the sound audible. Then, only, are you ready to relax and enjoy the program. When we relate to God in prayer, we must also eliminate all noises and distractions. Above all we must learn to listen with our undivided attention and with our whole being. Repeatedly in Sacred Scripture God begs us to listen. When we listen we are praying. Today Jesus says to us: "Listen carefully to this."

FIRST REFLECTION

v. 3 "Listen carefully to this."

Jesus invites us to listen. In these same words he is inviting us to pray. To listen is to pray. The word "listen," or one of its synonyms, is used frequently in Sacred Scripture. Since God never does anything without a purpose, he has a very definite reason for inviting us so frequently to listen. Listening is an art to be learned. Jesus invites us to listen carefully to what he wishes to communicate to us. He wants us to listen not

17

only with our ears, but to listen with our whole being. This is the gift of ourselves to God. Listening helps us arrive at that all-important prayer posture which says: "Here I am, Lord, what is it you want of me today?" (Listen to the Lord with your whole being.)

Colloquy: Lord, through your psalmist you advise me: "Be still and know that I am your God." Grant me the gift of stillness. Give me a listening heart that I may be open and receptive to what you want to accomplish in me and through me.

SECOND REFLECTION

vv. 4 & 15 "Some of what he sowed landed on the footpath, where the birds came along and ate it."

This is a simple description of the process of plowing and planting in Palestine. The footpath is not a highway nor even a road. It is a path on which the soil has been trodden hard. Since most of the traveling was done on foot, many of the paths cut through fields in various directions to make the shortest possible distance between two points. We too can become hardened like the footpaths as we are bombarded by the concerns of daily living, by our preoccupations with programs and projects in which we have become involved, by our inability or our unwillingness to set these aside in order to listen to what God is saying to us.

When we hear a word from God we do not always give it our full attention. The evil one is quick to carry the seed away by reminding us of the "all-important" concerns we have in life. Again we must analyze our priorities. How easily the preoccupations of every day take our focus off our true priority and deafen our sense of listening. (Be so still so that you can almost hear the seed growing.)

Colloquy: Lord, you speak to me in countless ways

each day. I miss your communication so often because I am not attuned to your wavelength. May I heed your psalmist when he says to me: "O, that today you would hear his voice; harden not your hearts."

THIRD REFLECTION

vv. 5-6 & 16-17 "Some of the seed landed on rocky ground where it had little soil . . . it began to wither for lack of roots."

What a simple metaphor, but how telling! We want to be accepted; we want to be loved. How difficult it is for us to accept criticism and persecution! Jesus warned us that if we are going to be his followers, we will be persecuted. In fact he said: "Blest are you when they insult you and persecute you . . . Be glad and rejoice." St. Paul also reminds us: "We are fools on Christ's account . . ." When our roots are deeply imbedded in God's love we will not wither.

When we have the mind of Christ then we will not be shaken by misunderstandings and persecution. Those who do not have the mind of Jesus will falter "when some pressure or persecution overtakes them because of the word." A tree blown by the wind imbeds its roots deep into the soil and becomes a sturdy tree. Persecution, likewise, strengthens us. (Be for the Lord and let him be for you.)

Colloquy: May my roots go deep in your love, Lord. Nourish me with your divine life so that I may not waver when persecution comes my way. Rather teach me to "be glad and rejoice."

FOURTH REFLECTION

vv. 7 & 18-19 "Again, some landed among thorns, which grew up and choked it off, and there was no yield of grain."

What a great privilege and gift is ours to have and know the Word of God! None of the pagan gods ever communicated with their devotees, but our loving Father began his communication with us through Abraham, Moses and the prophets. What is more, that Word has been preserved for us and placed at our very fingertips. What hope and encouragement, what assurance and comfort his Word brings us. How often we have the privilege to hear the Word of God in the Liturgy of the Mass, in our reading and study, in our prayer. Yet how often it has been choked off in our lives. Unfortunately, we live in the polluted atmosphere of secularism, materialism and humanism—all of which have choked off his Word. Unless his Word finds a home in our hearts, we will not be able to bear fruit. (Pause and listen.)

Colloquy: Lord, grant me the gift of detachment from "the desire for wealth and cravings of other sorts" so that your Word may not return to you void, but shall accomplish your will achieving the end for which you sent it.

FIFTH REFLECTION

v. 9 "Having spoken this parable, he added: 'Let him who has ears to hear me, hear!' "

Before Jesus began this parable he asked us to "listen carefully." Once again before he begins his explanation of the parable, he asks us to come with a listening heart. Listening is such an important prayer posture. God does not force himself upon us. He patiently waits for us to calm ourselves, to be still. So frequently we come to God with all our needs, our desires, our problems. As long as the focus in prayer is on ourselves, we will never be able to enter into a deep personal relationship with our Father nor will we come to a rich awareness of his presence within us and his love for us. We need to look beyond ourselves to keep our attention riveted upon our Father, our Abba, so that he can fill us with a more profound appreciation of his abiding love.

When we spend time listening in prayer, we give God a chance to mold, form and transform us into the kind of person he wants us to be.

Listening gives him a chance to fill us with his love. Listening also helps us to comprehend a little better that gracious and tremendous mystery which is God. (Rest quietly with the awareness of the Lord's presence within you.)

Colloquy: Abba, you urge me through your psalmist to "wait in patience and know that I am your God." Rid me of all the mundane concerns and distractions which crowd my mind and heart. Teach me how to empty myself so that you can fill me with your love, peace and joy.

SIXTH REFLECTION

v. 11 "To you the mystery of the reign of God has been confided."

Jesus was speaking to a crowd which had its own idea of the Kingdom of God. They lived with the expectation that a great Messiah would free them from the domination of Rome and establish a powerful, lasting earthly kingdom such as they enjoyed a thousand years before under King David. Repeatedly Jesus tried to eradicate this notion of a temporal kingdom, but they did not hear him. They would not permit themselves to be influenced by the possibility of a spiritual kingdom. The Twelve were beginning to comprehend what Jesus was saying; the rest were not. Jesus began to teach in elementary terms and by use of parables, hoping to convince them that his kingdom was a spiritual kingdom. We often find ourselves in the same frame of mind. We do not understand God's plans and his will in the events of our daily living. We sometimes lose our focus on our final destiny and God's design for attaining our total union with him. We need to listen attentively to his teaching in the parables. (Listen with every fibre of your being.)

Colloquy: Jesus, how patiently and persistently you taught. Through your Word you are trying to mold my thinking today, but how slow I am to comprehend. Thank you for your patient and enduring love in dealing with my slowness of heart.

SEVENTH REFLECTION

vv. 8 & 20 "Some seed, finally, landed on good soil and yielded grain that sprang up to produce at a rate of thirty- and sixty- and a hundredfold."

As we reflect on this parable are we not concerned about the category into which we fit? If we can see ourselves at times in the first class (the seed on the pathway), or in the second (on rocky ground), or in the third category (among thorns), then we should rejoice because we are no doubt the good soil which is producing a harvest in varying degrees. If we were not concerned about our receptivity to the Word of God, then we would have reason to be concerned. The Word of God is a powerful word. As we pray with the Word of God each day, we will find inspiration and motivation for our daily living. Life will not be humdrum, but we will discover a new exuberance about living. Likewise a conversion will gradually and painlessly take place within us as we expose our thinking to his Word. Furthermore, a transformation will be effected by his Word. We will discover a greater joy, a deeper peace in our lives. We will discover that we are lovable and then we will more easily be able to love others. That is the harvest his Word produces within us. (Spend the next moments quietly being with the Lord.)

Colloquy: Jesus, your Word is a powerful word, but ever so gentle. I must be open and pliable to it before it can produce a rich harvest within me. Grant me the grace to become loose soil to receive the seed of your Word so that together we may produce a rich harvest.

The following scriptural passages are offered, if you wish to pray longer with this theme:

I Samuel 3:1-10   "Speak, Lord, for your servant is listening. . . ."

Matthew 11:28-30   "Come to me, all you who are weary. . . ."

Revelation 3:14-22   "Here I stand, knocking at the door. . . ."

Psalm 95:1-11   "O, that today you would hear his voice:. . . ."

Matthew 13:4-23   ". . . a farmer went out sowing. . . ."

2 And God Saw That It Was Very Good

I Love You With A Creative Love
Psalm 104

Our astronauts have brought us to a deeper appreciation of the beauty of God's creation both by their enthusiastic verbal descriptions as well as by their magnificent photographs. The Book of Genesis describes God's creation in brief, factual statements while the psalmist sings of creation as the manifestation of God's love. The psalmist describes the world as he saw it. We know the world as much more complex; nevertheless, we can take equal delight in God's creative love. Psalm 104 is a hymn of praise to God our Creator. It is one of the most remarkable songs in the Psalter. God lives in and loves every aspect of the world he created. Each one of the seven parts of the Psalm can be used as a springboard into prayer for each day of a week.

FIRST REFLECTION

vv. 1-4 ". . . You are clothed in majesty and glory, robed in light as with a cloak. . . ."

God is transcendent. We cannot begin to fathom his glory and majesty. We only get a tiny glimpse of his transcendence as manifested in the works of his creation. We stand in awe and reverence as we gaze upon his mighty power so evident in the works of his hands.

God is present in his creation "robed in light as with

a cloak." In Sacred Scripture light is a symbol of God's presence. His presence is verbally portrayed as a brilliant, luminous light. It is not a frightening nor annoying light, but rather awe-inspiring, peaceful and inviting. Jesus said: "I am the light of the world. No follower of mine shall ever walk in darkness; no, he shall possess the light of life" *John 8:12*. (Spend some time basking in the sunshine of his presence or enjoy the twinkling stars or the beauty of the moon.)

Colloquy: I praise you, Father, present in the heavenly palace which you created. Teach me to stand in awe and reverence of your creative love so that I may respond in love.

SECOND REFLECTION

vv. 5-9 "You fixed the earth upon its foundation, not to be moved forever; . . ."

God brought into existence the totality of creation—the earth, the sea, the mountains. He created everything by a simple act of his will. The figurative language and the images used in Scripture help us to rise from the mundane to the "otherness" of the Creator. God not only created the world, but he continues to sustain it as he spans the mountains and tames the oceans. Even though we stand in awe at the immensity of the universe and the power reflected in the mountains and oceans, today let us reflect on the transcendence of God's creative power as evident in the mobility of an ant, the fragrance of a rose, the smile of a child, the dexterity of our hands, and the myriad other wonders of his creation. (Be alone with your God as you reflect on a special work of his creation.)

Colloquy: Father, the tops of the mountains are yours. In spirit let me climb a mountain today to rise above the mundane and ordinary cares of life to discover more clearly your presence and your love.

THIRD REFLECTION

vv. 10-18 "You send forth springs into the watercourses that wind among the mountains, . . ."

How lovingly God cares for all his creatures — wild asses, birds of heaven, cattle, man himself! Life-giving water is God's gift provided for his creatures wherever they may be. In his loving concern he provides. When we suffer from thirst we can appreciate more fully his gift of water. How meticulously God provided water for every need. Today, immerse yourself in a beautiful scene of God's creation. In spirit see the beasts, birds, bread, wine, oil, goats, men—all the work of his hand; all cared for by the water he provides. (Rest quietly in God's presence with your eyes closed and listen to the water flowing—a babbling brook, a gentle rain, a mighty waterfall.)

Colloquy: Jesus, you gave me the living waters of your divine life dwelling within me. Just as fresh water is essential for my physical life, so your living water is absolutely indispensable for my spiritual life. I praise you with all my being.

FOURTH REFLECTION

vv. 19-23 "You made the moon to mark the seasons; the sun knows the hour of its setting. . . ."

The sun, moon and stars are another area of the mighty creation of God. The psalmist looks at various phases of God's creation to help us fathom the immensity of God's creative power. As we gaze upon the light—the sun, moon and stars—we can begin to comprehend the vastness and profundity of God's creative genius. God takes delight in his creation and the works of his hands delight in him. As the prophet puts it: "Before whom the stars at their posts shine and rejoice; when he calls them, they answer, 'Here we are!' shining with joy for their Maker. Such is our God; no other is to be compared to him" (*Baruch 3:34ff*). Isn't this a delightful image? Can't you see the stars wiggling in their joy and dancing like happy little children? (In spirit, or in reality, gaze at the stars and let the starlight touch your heart.)

Colloquy: Loving Abba, let my heart dance with joy as I contemplate the beauty of your creative love. I want to praise and thank you all the days of my life.

FIFTH REFLECTION

vv. 24-26 "How manifold are your works, O Lord. . . ."

Stand on the beach today in spirit or in actuality. Let the vast expanse of water, the thundering of the waves, "the sea . . . great and wide . . . living things both small and great" speak to your heart of the Creator who brought all this into existence. Let the roar of the water drown out all other distracting sounds and let its roar become a paean of praise to our creative Father. Each facet of his creation brings us to a deeper sense of awe and reverence. (Let your gaze reach beyond the immensity of the sea and reach out to your God.)

Colloquy: Lord, as I gaze upon your ocean it reminds me of the immensity of the ocean of your love for me. It is boundless; it is inexhaustible. Father, even though my love may be like a tiny drop of water as compared with the ocean of your love, please accept it in return for the limitless love you have showered upon me throughout my whole life.

SIXTH REFLECTION

vv. 27-30 "They all look to you to give them food in due time. . . ."

God, our loving Father, is the source of my life. The Father breathes life into all his creatures. He continues to sustain life: "If you take away their breath, they perish and return to dust." In his loving concern, the Father created the sources of food which the earth produces so abundantly season after season. God also created the oxygen which sustains our life. The air we breathe symbolizes the Holy Spirit who is the source of the divine life dwelling within us. In Scripture he is called a breath, a gentle breeze, a mighty wind. Thus the psalmist prays: "When you send forth your spirit, they are created, and you renew the face of the earth. (Relax and concentrate on your breathing. Instead of oxygen think of breathing in God's divine life.)

Colloquy: Father, I praise and thank you for the magnificent creative power. I thank you for endowing me with life and the faculties to recognize and rejoice in your creative love. Teach me to love you in return.

SEVENTH REFLECTION

vv. 31-35 "May the glory of the Lord endure forever; may the Lord be glad in his works. . . ."

When we behold the creative love of God we become more and more aware of his transcendent and majestic power. He fashioned the creatures he loves and the world for us with every minute detail. God takes delight in his creation. His joy pervades all his works. Our prime duty is to praise and glorify our loving Creator who is our Father and our Abba. The psalmist invites us to join him as he prays: "I will sing to the Lord all my life; I will sing praise to my God while I live." (Rest in his presence and let your heart sing his praises.)

Colloquy: Father, your creative love simply overwhelms me as I ponder the marvels of your creation. With the psalmist I say: "Bless the Lord, O my soul! Alleluia."

Here are a few additional scriptural passages which remind us of God's creative love.

Isaiah 43:1-5   "I have called you by name: you are mine. . . ."

Isaiah 49:1-16	"See, upon the palms of my hands I have written your name. . . ."
Psalm 139:1-24	"Truly you have formed me my inmost being; you knit me in my mother's womb. . . ."
John 15:1-17	"There is no greater love than this: to lay down one's life for one's friends. . . ."

3 Wonder, Awe, Reverence

Our Majestic God
Sirach 17:1-27

At an informal social gathering a friend of mine, an obstetrician by profession, was asked if he believed in miracles. He looked up with a quiet smile and replied: "I see them every day." A mother of seven expressed the same truth: "Each time I hold my newborn babe in my arms for the first time, I can just feel the presence and the power of God. It is a rich contemplative experience for me." How true! Every birth is another expression of God's creative love. The author of the Book of Sirach describes God's wisdom in creating the universe and everything in it. He tells us that God created people in his own image. He endowed them "with power over all things else on earth" and "set before them knowledge." Furthermore, God created us "to praise his holy name." We must render an account of our deeds to God. Even a casual reflection on God's almighty, creating power fills us with awe, reverence and wonder. Listen intently with your whole being to what God is saying to you through the works of his creation.

FIRST REFLECTION

vv. 1-4 "The Lord from the earth created man, and in his own image he made him. . . ."
All of creation reflects the divine wisdom of God. As

we ponder God's creative genius we are astounded at the order and design which we find in all his works. Undoubtedly rational man is the crown of God's creation. God gifted his creature man with intelligence and free will. He gave man power over much of his creation. This is an awesome privilege. God did even more for man: "Any who did accept him, he empowered to become children of God" (John 1:12). Yes, our loving Father shares his divine life with us even in this land of exile. This fact sweetens our alienation from God and is a foretaste of our more complete participation in his divine life prepared for us for all eternity. In order to reach this goal, "limited days of life he gives him and makes him return to earth again." (Be still and know that he is God.)

Colloquy: Father, thank you for calling me into existence and endowing me with immortality to be with you forever. I praise you for the marvelous wonders and exquisite beauty of your creation. May each day bring me to a richer awareness of what you have prepared for those who love you.

SECOND REFLECTION

vv. 5-8 "He looks with favor upon their hearts, and
      shows them his glorious works, . . ."

Man's first and greatest privilege is to contemplate "the wonders of his deeds and to praise his holy name." Stand beside your heavenly Father, let him show you all of his creation and listen to him as he asks: "What more could I have done for you and have not done it?" "He forms men's tongues and eyes and ears." Reflect momentarily on your eyes. You can see the stars countless miles away as well as read the printed page before you. There was no focusing or readjusting necessary on your part. So wonderful is your gift of sight. Recall too the beautiful things you have enjoyed with your gift of vision, a towering mountain, a gorgeous rose, an exquisite sunset, as well as the joy dancing in the eyes of a child. Try to answer your loving Abba as he asks, "What more could I have done for you?" (Let his question sink into the depths of your being.)

Colloquy: Father, you are the transcendent God of heaven and earth, the Creator of the entire universe, yet you have created me and endowed me with the gift of speech, the ability to hear, the facility to see. For all this I praise your holy name.

THIRD REFLECTION

vv. 9-10 "An everlasting covenant he has made with them, . . ."

God has set before us the "law of life" and "his commandments he has revealed to them." God's laws are not rules and regulations curtailing our liberty. Rather they are a covenant binding us together as his special people. As St. Peter reminds us: "You, however, are 'a chosen race, a royal priesthood, a holy nation, a people he claims for his own to proclaim [his] glorious works' " (*I Peter 2:9*). He loves us with an infinite love, hence he wants us to be closely united with him for all eternity. This is the highest level of love—to be united with the person loved, to be part of his life, his hopes and sorrows, his joys and happiness. How overwhelming is the mystery of that love! How unfathomable! Yet our loving Father says to us: "You are precious in my sight and I love you." What joy to know that we are loved! (Let this truth touch your heart.)

Colloquy: Loving Father, words fail me; I am speechless as I bask in the sunshine of your love! Let me linger in your presence and experience your love for me. Help me to say "I love you, too."

FOURTH REFLECTION

vv. 11-13 "His majestic glory their eyes beheld, his glorious voice their ears heard. . . ."

Our finite minds cannot possibly grasp the majesty of our glorious God. When we seem to gain just a little insight into his majesty he completely escapes us. He does give us just a little glimpse into his beauty as we stand in awe at a celestial sunset, or the rugged beauty of a huge mountain, or the intricate artistry of a flower, or the mystery of an atom.

We sometimes hear his "glorious voice" not verbally but with our whole being as we sense his presence, or feel his love, or are touched deep down inside at the very core of our being. His very goodness draws us. His almighty power staggers our imagination. His personal love envelops us. (Rest in his love and let it warm your heart.)

Colloquy: Lord, you are the God of might and power, the Lord of heaven and earth, the Creator of all that is, yet I dare to call you "Father"; even more, I call you "Abba."

FIFTH REFLECTION

vv. 14-18 ". . . the Lord's own portion is Israel. . . ."

How often the Father says to us in the Old Testament: "You will be my people and I will be your God." In our own day God has invited us through our Baptism to become a member of his family. He adopts us as his sons and daughters. He shares with us his divine life. Paul says: "All who are led by the Spirit of God are sons of God . . . a spirit of adoption through which we cry out 'Abba' " (*Rom. 8:14*). Or again in Isaiah: "Fear not, for I have redeemed you; I have called you by name: you are mine" (*Isaiah 43:1*). And God fulfills that promise: "This is God's dwelling among men. He shall dwell with them and they shall be his people and he shall be their God who is always with them" (*Rev. 21:3*). Since God is our loving Father we are "the Lord's portion." We belong to him. What greater privilege could be ours! (Pause and listen.)

Colloquy: Father, how can I thank you for inviting me into your family? Help me to express my gratitude by living up to the dignity which you gave me. May I be a worthy child of my Father and may I reflect your goodness all the days of my life.

SIXTH REFLECTION

vv. 19-25 "To the penitent he provides a way back, he encourages those who are losing hope!"

Our loving Father in effect says to us: "I don't care what you have done, I love you anyway." He also says to us: "I myself will look after and tend my sheep. . . . The lost I will seek out, the strayed I will bring back, the injured I will bind up, the sick I will heal" (*Ezekiel 34:11 & 16*). Jesus spent his whole public life in loving concern for the lost sheep, those who had separated themselves from God.

Reflect on Jesus' reaching out with merciful love to the sinful woman (Luke 7) and to the adulteress (John 8) as well as in the three parables of mercy (Luke 15), not to mention his promise to the Good Thief: "I assure you: this day you will be with me in paradise" (*Luke 23:43*). Jesus personalized his forgiveness and healing for each one of us when he instituted the Sacrament of Reconciliation (*John 20:19-23*). From personal experience I am sure we can say with the sacred writer: "To the penitent he provides a way back. . . ." (Permit his forgiving love to envelop you.)

Colloquy: O Lord, how consoling to know that your love will never change regardless of my sinfulness, my weakness, my lack of generosity, my half-hearted response to your love. As I ponder your mercy and compassion, make me totally receptive to your love and help me respond with a more generous love.

SEVENTH REFLECTION

vv. 26-27 "Is anything brighter than the sun? . . . God

watches over the hosts of highest
heaven. . . ."

Our minds cannot possibly grasp the immensity, the
power and the beauty of God. Much less can we find
words to describe his transcendence. We simply stand
in awe and reverence, in wonder and amazement. The
inspired author himself cannot express what he is experiencing. He begins to compare the brilliance of God
with the brightness of the sun, but immediately rejects
the illustration because the sun has already been
eclipsed by the presence and power of God. God is the
Lord "over the hosts of highest heaven," yet he is our
Father. He is a loving Abba who is concerned about
even the number of hairs on our head. He wants to give
us his love, his peace and his joy if we are open to
receive these gifts. He does call us back to "dust and
ashes" but only that we might be united with him for
all eternity. His love for us is so great that he cannot be
separated from us. "How deep are the riches and the
wisdom and the knowledge of God! How inscrutable
his judgments, how unsearchable his ways!" (*Romans*
11:33). (Be quiet in the wonder of his love.)

Colloquy: Lord, how overwhelming is the very
thought of your presence and power, your forgiving
and enduring love! What can I say except I adore you, I
worship you, I love you as a Father?

The psalms are inspired prayers of praise, wonder,
awe and reverence of God. Here are a few suggestions
for further prayer on this theme. God's providence and
care: Psalms 1; 4; 5; 16; 21; 23; 33; 91; 127; 139.
Trust in God who protects us: Psalms 27; 46; 62; 125; 1-2.
Reverence and praise: Psalms 34; 84.
Praise of God: Psalms 8; 18; 19; 24; 30; 33; 34; 47; 65; 67;
89; 90; 93; 95; 96; 97; 98; 100; 103; 104; 111; 113; 115; 116;
118; 121; 139; 145; 146; 147; 148; 150.

4 More Than Many Sparrows

The Father Loves You With a Providing Love
Matthew 6: 25-34

Repeatedly my Mother would calm my childish anxieties and worries with the axiom: "Today is the tomorrow that you were worrying about yesterday, but it didn't happen." How much truth there is in that adage, yet how difficult it is for us to recall it at the crucial moments in our lives. Jesus reminds us of the caring, providing love of the Father for us, then he says bluntly: "Stop worrying!" As we contemplate our loving Abba's providential care and concern for us, even to his awareness of every hair on our head, then we will begin to form an attitude of trust and confidence. Gradually we will be able to let go and accept willingly and completely whatever plans God has for us. This transformation will dispel all undue fear, worry and anxiety from our hearts.

As we listen to what Jesus is saying to us in the above passage, we will begin to experience that transformation taking place within us. We will begin to trust implicitly and eventually to abandon ourselves totally to our loving Father's will and his plan for us. (Before you begin your prayer, read the whole Scriptural passage slowly and reflectively, permitting every word to sink in.)

FIRST REFLECTION

v. 25 "Is not the body more valuable than clothes?"

Our body is the masterpiece of God's creation. Reflect momentarily on some parts of your body. Observe the dexterity of your hand. It is capable of doing the most delicate work and also strong enough for heavy manual work. Your eyes can see an object close by as well as something at a considerable distance without any noticeable focusing. Our ears enjoy the sound of music, the songs of the birds as well as words of endearment and encouragement from those who love us. Touch and taste are gifts provided by our loving Creator. Above all this, our body is the temple of the Holy Spirit dwelling within us. How precious it is! (Let this truth sink down to the core of your being.)

Colloquy: Father, I am your work of art, a masterpiece of your creation. With a sustaining, providing, caring love you grant me every heartbeat so that I may enjoy the gift of life and all that it entails. Thank you, Father.

SECOND REFLECTION

v. 26 "Look at the birds in the sky. . . ."

What a delight the birds of the air bring us, from the soaring of an eagle to the chirping of a sparrow! They express their praise to their Creator from the melodious song of the canary to the doleful mourning of the dove. Our loving Father has provided their plumage with its delicate shading of feathers and richness of color. What awe and reverence they inspire in us as we watch them build their nests and provide for their young. How minutely, how intricately our loving Father has provided for all his creatures. (Quietly watch a bird.)

Colloquy: Father as I reflect upon the birds of the air, I am reminded how lavishly you have provided for me. I am overwhelmed at your loving care and concern. Teach me to be grateful.

THIRD REFLECTION

v.27 "Which of you by worrying can add a moment to his lifespan?"

Every breath is another expression of God's providential love. Life itself is a free gift from our loving Father. He wants us to enjoy every moment of life filled with his countless blessings. His blessings are not merely temporal. Jesus tells us: "I came that they might have life and have it to the full" (John 10:10). This divine life which we will enjoy for all eternity is his special gift to us. If this greatest of all gifts is given to us why should we worry? Why should we want to add a moment to our life-span, knowing that a life of infinite bliss is awaiting us? (Pause to breathe in this divine life.)

Colloquy: Jesus by your passion, death and resurrection you filled me with your divine life. What dignity is mine! Keep me open and receptive to the infilling of your divine presence. May it truly be a foretaste of my total union with you.

FOURTH REFLECTION

v.28 "Learn a lesson from the way the wild flowers grow. . . ."

A desert flower may never be seen by man, nevertheless, it sends its fragrance and beauty up to God. How often we have enjoyed a hillside carpeted with the radiant array of variegated color created by our provident Father. Perhaps we have had the privilege to find a flower on a mountain top showing forth its beautiful bloom through a blanket of snow. All this beauty has been bestowed on us by our loving Abba. How graciously he provides the warm sun, the gentle rain, the rich earth, the nurturing atmosphere to these delicate plants so that his love might be reflected in them and that we may enjoy them. (Prayerfully study a flower.)

Colloquy: Father, open my heart so that I may enjoy the splendor of these works of your hands. Teach me to raise my heart in joyful thanks and praise as I drink in their beauty.

FIFTH REFLECTION

vv. 29-32 "O weak in faith! . . . Your heavenly Father knows all that you need."

How important to Jesus was the faith of his followers. He was visibly pleased when he found faith, but registered disappointment at the lack of it. Listen to Jesus say: "Have faith in God and faith in me" *(John 14:1)* or again "Your faith has restored you to health" *(Matthew 9:22)*. Our heavenly Father is a provident Father. He does not begrudgingly dole out what we need. On the contrary his infinite love is constantly supplying us with a superabundance for our needs. He loves to hear us ask him for what we need because then we manifest our poverty of spirit and show our total dependence upon him. (Rest in your Father's arms.)

Colloquy: Father, grant me the gift of unwavering, expectant faith knowing that you will care for my every need—physical, spiritual, psychological. Teach me to trust you.

SIXTH REFLECTION

v. 33 "Seek first his kingship over you, his way of holiness, and all these things will be given you besides."

When Jesus invites us to seek first his kingship over us, he is asking us to raise our focus above ourselves and above all the neon gods which creep into our lives. Focusing on self in the whirlwind of activities which plague our lives causes fears, doubts, tensions. If we keep our focus on our loving Father, our lives will have a real sense of direction. All the other mundane preoccupations become so peripheral and unimportant. Our provident Father reminds us that he loves us when he says: "I know well the plans I have in mind for you . . . plans for your welfare, not for woe." His providential love not only has plans for us, but his love also supplies the means to implement those plans if we but trust him. (Rest in his presence and let him love you.)

Colloquy: Jesus, you had one set purpose during your earthly sojourn and that was to do the will of your Father. You were singleminded in that purpose. Grant me the insight and generosity to want what you, Father, want of me.

SEVENTH REFLECTION

v. 34 "Enough, then, of worrying about tomorrow. Let tomorrow take care of itself. . . ."

There is one all-important moment in our lives which is precious to God and that is this present moment. We even call it the sacrament of the moment. Jesus advises us not to worry, but to trust. There is a great difference between worry and concern. Worry is that undue anxiety which robs us of our peace. Once we experience the love of God for us, then we can trust implicitly. (Abandon yourself totally to your Father and rest quietly in that thought.)

Colloquy: Father, I place myself totally in your hands knowing that your love will care for me every moment of the day. Banish all anxiety and worry from my heart.

Additional suggested scriptural passages for your prayer with this theme of God's providential love:

Jeremiah 29: 11-14	"For I know well the plans I have in mind for you. . . ."
John 3: 16-17	"Yes, God so loved the world that he gave his only Son. . . ."
Ephesians: 2: 1-10	"God is rich in mercy; because of his great love for us he brought us to life with Christ when we were dead in sin. . . ."

Romans 8: 28-34	"We know that God makes all things work together for the good of those who have been called according to his decree. . . ."
Psalm 100: 1-4	"Know that the Lord is God. . . ."
Psalm 136: 1-26	"Give thanks to the Lord, for he is good. . . ."

5 Why Did You Do Such a Thing?

God Complains About Man's Unfaithfulness
Genesis 3: 1-24

Listen to God complain about the unfaithfulness, the sinfulness of man as he refused to return the love of his Creator! Does that statement startle you? The possibility of an all-powerful God complaining may seem rather preposterous. Admittedly we are speaking anthropomorphically, nonetheless God's complaining does illustrate his great love for us. God loves us so much that he is disappointed when we refuse to love him in return. God complains because man, by his sinfulness, brings upon himself misery, pain, suffering, unhappiness.

As we pray with the following Scripture and as we listen to God's complaint we can comprehend more fully the mystery of his overwhelming love for us.

FIRST REFLECTION

v. 1 "Did God really tell you not to eat from any of the trees in the garden?"

Listen carefully to this question of the serpent. Immediately you can detect his subtle intrigue, his cynical mentality, his diabolic deception. Eve attempts to answer his question graciously and tries to explain that they may eat of all the trees in the garden except one. Already she is being taken in. She should never have deigned to recognize, much less, answer the serpent. From our vantage point in history, we can more easily discern the machinations of the evil one as he confronts Eve. Unsuspectingly Eve is being deceived because she was flattered by the thought: "You will be like gods." The evil one has lost none of his cunning, nor are we, with our human nature weakened by sin, any better prepared to recognize his wiles. Our own record speaks for itself. In spite of our naivety, and our frequent falls, God continues to come to us in the cool of the evening. (Reflect for a few moments on your own record and God's fidelity.)

Colloquy: Come, O Holy Spirit, endow me with your gifts of wisdom, knowledge, understanding and discernment so that I may recognize the subtleties of the evil one in my life. Strengthen me to be loyal, receptive and responsive to your voiceless voice within me.

SECOND REFLECTION

v. 6 "The woman saw that the tree was good for food, pleasing to the eyes, and desirable for gaining wisdom."

In this brief statement we find a temptation to several of the capital sins. The devil is cunning and clever enough to represent sin and evil as something good and desirable. Here the devil ingeniously and slyly appeals to Eve's appetite: "the tree was good for food," to her sense of sight: "pleasing to the eyes," and to her pride: "desirable for gaining wisdom." The evil one knows the woman's vulnerability. Gradually Eve is losing her focus on the number one priority in her life—her loving Creator and Father. How quickly she forgets his creative and providential love! A momentary reflection should have reminded her of God's great love for her. He wanted only her happiness. As her focus became more self-centered, her fall was becoming more imminent. (Be alone in the presence of your Creator.)

44

Colloquy: Compassionate Father, I find myself in this same pattern so many times. Help me to keep my focus on you and you alone. Forgive the many times I have strayed. How comforting to know that you love me in spite of my sinfulness.

THIRD REFLECTION

v. 6 "So she took some of its fruit and ate it; and she also gave some to her husband, who was with her, and he ate it."

This simple statement records a wilful act of man in refusing to obey his God, an act which he hoped would make him like God. The dire consequences of this first sin have reverberated in every corner of the world ever since. Its consequences have inflicted the heart of every person ever born into this life, save one. This deliberate refusal to accept God has wrought an infinite chasm, a breach between man and his loving Creator. He deprived man of the great gift God wanted to give him, the gift of himself in the bliss of heaven for all eternity. Little wonder that God complained! (Listen to God!)

Colloquy: O God, sin is a refusal to love, to return your gracious love. How often I have refused! How often I have caused you to complain! I offer my pittance of love in reparation for the sins that are being committed at this very moment.

FOURTH REFLECTION

v. 9 "Where are you?"

What a plaintive call coming from a God who loves! Man has rebelled against his God. Man has said by his deliberate choice and action: "I will not serve." How does God react? Our loving Father goes in search of man. God could have totally annihilated man, but instead he seeks out his creature and pleads with him: "Where are you? Where are you in your relationship to me? Where are you in your own estimation now that you have rebelled?" Yet God continues to search, to seek out, to call "Come back to me." That is the mystery of God! That kind of love makes sin imcomprehensible, yet man continues to sin and God continues to love. (Listen to God say to you, "Where are you?")

Colloquy: Father, how continuously mankind turns away from you and refuses to acknowledge you the Creator of the universe. How many times I join my voice with theirs in refusing to love. "Where are you?" I hear you say. Yes, we have misery, war, injustice, famine and the manifold inflictions which we have brought on ourselves. Father, please accept our apologies.

FIFTH REFLECTION

v. 10 & 11 "I was afraid . . . ."
"You have eaten, then, from the tree of which I had forbidden you to eat!"

Tragedy has struck. The fruit which seemed so good for food, so pleasing to the eye and so desirable for gaining wisdom has now turned to bitter sorrow and confusion. The apparent palatable fruit left nothing but ashes of disillusionment in the mouth. Fear is the result of sin. God is a God of love, but sin makes us afraid. By sinning we have refused to love and now find ourselves afraid as love approaches. The first sin caused man to try to hide from God; it has done the same throughout the ages. Life without God is hell. God is the only source of happiness, peace and joy. "The wages of sin is death." (Just be there.)

Colloquy: Loving Father, fear dominates the hearts of so many of your people. They continue to turn from you, the only souce of love. Touch their hearts and minds and grant them the grace to return to you.

SIXTH REFLECTION

v. 13 "Why did you do such a thing?"

The tragic disappointment which this question embodies is not only addressed to the woman but to all of us each time we fail to love. When we sin we rationalize and justify our actions. We can find dozens of excuses just as the first man did. God reaches out to us by asking: "Why did you do such a thing?" He wants us to pause and refocus our thoughts. He asks this question to bring us to a humble admission of our weakness and infidelity so that sorrow may fill our hearts. Only then can he lavish his total forgiveness upon us. (Try to answer God's inquiry in your own heart.)

Colloquy: Father, my pattern in life is so similar to that of Adam and Eve. I fail you, then I try to justify what I have done. Move me to genuine sorrow that I may enjoy your loving compassion.

SEVENTH REFLECTION

v. 15 "I will put enmity between you and the woman. . . ."

What a mysterious God is our gracious Father! Man has utterly failed him, rebelled against him, refused his love. God's deep disappointment caused him to complain but his infinite love dominated as he promised man a redeemer who would once again establish a personal relationship between Creator and creature. Our compassionate Father says: "My heart is overwhelmed, my pity is stirred. I will not give vent to my blazing anger . . . for I am God and not man" *(Hosea 11:8f)*. This was the very first promise of a redeemer. Man must accept some of the consequences of his sin: "By the sweat of your face shall you get bread to eat." However, even these dreadful consequences are overshadowed by the hope of an eternal union of love with our loving Father. (Bask in the sunshine of that heavenly love.)

Colloquy: Father, your compassion overwhelms us as we reflect on our own infidelities, our sins, our deliberate refusal to accept your love. Yet, you continue to love us in spite of all we have done. Thank you for that love.

Some additional thoughts on sin and its consequences:

Death and Judgment:

Luke 12:16-21 Parable of the rich man

Matthew 16:24-28 What profit to gain the whole world?

Hell:

Matthew 7:13-28 "Enter through the narrow gate."

Matthew 25:1-13 Parable of the Ten Virgins

Reconciliation:

Ezekiel 36:24-27 "I will give you a new heart. . . ."

Luke 15:11-32 Prodigal Son

Romans 8:28-39 "Who will separate us from the love of Christ?"

6. Celebrate and Rejoice

*Listen to God Say: "I Don't Care What You Have Done.
I Love You Anyway"*
Luke 15:11-32

The movie *Fiesta* is a contemporary retelling of the Parable of the Prodigal Son. The older brother denounces his younger brother by saying to the father: "I have no brother." With great patience and compassion the father responds: "I have a riddle for you to solve. I have two sons. You are my son and yet you say you have no brother. How do you explain that?"

The question posed in that riddle may touch us at the very core of our being and most likely we will spontaneously ask ourselves if we have ever said: "I have no brother."

This scene portrays the mercy, compassion and forgiveness of a loving father. In thirty minutes the movie depicts many themes: reconciliation, family life, alienation, interpersonal relations, forgiveness. Dominating all these and making all the rest possible is God's forgiving, redeeming love. How incomprehensible is our Father's love for us!

FIRST REFLECTION

vv. 11-13 "Father, give me the share of the estate that is coming to me."

Selfishness is at the root of all sin. In this parable the selfishness of the younger brother surfaces. He does not consider whether or not he is needed at home, or if the father can afford to give him his inheritance at this time. He knew that according to the Law a father could abdicate before his death and divide his wealth. He took advantage of this Law. His selfishness plunged him into sins of unrestrained sensuality and spendthrift extravagance, according to the Greek word and according to the elder brother's statement in verse 30. Pleasure and self-gratification can never satisfy the human heart. How often this has been regrettably proven through the ages. (Pause, rest, reflect.)

Colloquy: Father, how frequently my selfishness has been the cause of my sin! I count on your grace to help me look beyond myself. Teach me to keep my gaze always riveted on you. Help me to rise above my selfishness and be concerned about others.

SECOND REFLECTION

vv. 14-16 "He was in dire need . . . He longed to fill his belly with the husks that were fodder for the pigs. . . ."

Self-gratification and pleasure can never fulfill the longing of our heart. How aptly St. Augustine says: "Our hearts are restless until they rest in Thee." How often sin leaves ashes of disillusionment in our mouths. The human heart hungers for the peace and joy which only God can give, but how frequently we take the wrong avenue to find it. How often we seek out the husks! Like pleasure they cannot satisfy the hunger of our hearts. (Pause and listen to what your heart desires.)

Colloquy: Jesus, you create in me a hunger and thirst for you. Direct my steps so that I can find satisfaction only in your will. Teach me to want what you want for me.

THIRD REFLECTION

vv. 17-19 "Coming to his senses at last, he said: ". . . I
will break away and return to my father. . . ."

God loves us with an infinite love. At times he may
use trials, hardships or suffering, which we mostly
inflict on ourselves, to bring us to our senses. Just as
hunger helped the young man come to his senses, so
difficulties help us arrive at a change of heart. Conversion begins with a change of heart which is then translated into resolution and action. "I will break away and
return to my father," is a resolution which required
courageous determination on the part of the younger
son. It also required humility. Without genuine poverty of spirit and humility, a conversion cannot be
authentic. (Be still and listen.)

Colloquy: Father, thank you for the example of the
younger son. How much I need that humility and
determination to turn away from my many weaknesses
and failures and to throw myself into your arms. Please
grant me that grace.

FOURTH REFLECTION

vv. 20-21 "While he was still a long way off, his
father caught sight of him and was deeply
moved. . . ."

What a touching picture of our heavenly Father! This
parable reveals the merciful, compassionate love of the
Father. The Father spent long days watching and waiting for the return of his son. How patiently our Father
in heaven waits for us! If we take but one tiny step
toward the Father, he immediately takes the other
ninety-nine to reach us. Listen to him say to us: "It is I, I
who wipe out, for my own sake, your offenses; your
sins I remember no more" *(Isaiah 43:25)*. It is hard for us
to comprehend that kind of gracious, forgiving love.
Our minds simply cannot fathom it. What joy, what
peace, what reassurance it brings to us. (Forgive yourself.)

Colloquy: Father, I have failed you so many times. In my pride, I am so apt to become discouraged, but your loving compassion bouys me up. Thank you for loving me with a forgiving, healing, redeeming love.

FIFTH REFLECTION

vv. 22-4 "Let us eat and celebrate. . . ."

The compassionate father does not reluctantly forgive his son and begrudgingly accept him as a servant as the son requested. The robe, the ring and the shoes are all symbols of forgiveness, acceptance and reinstatement into the family circle. The past is gone forever. All that is important is the sacrament of the moment, and this moment was one of a great outpouring of love. Are these symbols of acceptance—the robe, the ring and shoes—not reminiscent of the wedding garment which Jesus spoke about? Is not the celebration a foretaste of the heavenly banquet which we will enjoy as we are united with the Father? What an overwhelming Love! (Be alone with God and thank him for loving you.)

Colloquy: Father, the mystery of your loving compassion overwhelms me. I too must confess: "Father I have sinned against you," but how consoling to know that your merciful love blots out all my sinfulness and your love for me continues just the same.

SIXTH REFLECTION

vv. 25-30 "I have slaved for you. . . ."

In his anger the true nature of the elder son betrays itself. His work at home was not a labor of love. It did not arise from a sense of duty to father and family. He even considered it slavery. In other words, he was working out of sheer necessity to acquire his patrimony. Notice too that the elder brother was well aware of what his younger brother was doing, but there is no indication that he tried to save him from himself. The sins of the younger brother were sins of human weakness. Even though they might have been grave, there was no malice in them. The same cannot be said of the elder brother. His refusal to forgive, his refusal to accept his younger brother in love, betrayed the hardness of heart which Jesus lamented so many times. (Listen to your heart say: I forgive.)

Colloquy: Jesus, how often I play the role of the elder brother as I sit in judgment on others! How slow I am to forgive and forget! I fervently pray: "Forgive us our trespasses as we forgive those who trespass against us."

SEVENTH REFLECTION

vv. 31-32 "We had to celebrate and rejoice! . . ."

Can we not identify with the elder brother? We are the elder brother in many ways. What is our personal reaction toward sinners? This parable is unfinished. We would like to know what happened to the elder brother. Did he finally accept his younger brother? Was there a change of heart? It is unfinished because the outcome depends on us. What is our reaction? Repentance always calls for joy, for a celebration. Did not Jesus say: "There will likewise be more joy in heaven over one repentant sinner than over ninety-nine righteous people who have no need to repent." There is another reason to celebrate. In spite of our waywardness, our weakness, our sinfulness, our Father continues to love us just the same. (Pause and let your heart dance.)

Colloquy: Jesus, teach me genuine sorrow for my sinfulness. Fill my heart with your love so that sin loses all of its attraction in my life. When I fail, move me to a humble admission and keep me *receptive to your forgiveness* and love.

We may approach this incident from another point of view. Since Jesus assumed the burden of our sinfulness by uniting himself with our human nature, he can be considered the wayward son. You may wish to contemplate this passage again, considering the burden of our sin laid upon Jesus and the Father's reaction to Jesus.

Additional passages revealing God's loving mercy and compassion:

Hosea—Chapters 2 and 11
Ezekiel 16:1-63
Isaiah 54:1-10
Luke 15:1-7
Luke 7:36-50
John 21:15-17
Psalms 103, 51, 32, 143

7 Gabriel Breaks the Good News

The Annunciation
Luke 1: 26-38

God is a God of surprises. We may ask for a certain favor only to discover that God outdoes himself in generosity. He may not grant the favor we ask, because his ways are not our ways, but he may grant us instead blessings so great that we would hesitate to ask for them. The Chosen People were expecting a redeemer who would restore their relationship with God. Little did they expect that God himself would assume a human nature and become their savior and ours. In fact, the thought was so preposterous that Jesus spent a lifetime trying to convince them that he was God. Listen with total and quiet receptivity to the unfolding of God's plans.

FIRST REFLECTION

v. 28 "Rejoice, O highly favored daughter! The Lord is with you. Blessed are you among women."

Mary did rejoice and so do we because God is faithful to his promises. He promised us a Savior and now his divine plan is beginning to unfold. "Yes, God so loved the world that he gave his only Son" (*John 3:16*). Because of her sinlessness the Lord is with Mary in a unique way. God is our loving Father, we are his children. Mary is the daughter of the Father, the Mother of the Son and the Spouse of the Holy Spirit. Mary did rejoice not only because of her singular role especially chosen by God, but because God was saving his people. (Let your heart rejoice.)

Colloquy: Father, how much reason I have to rejoice and celebrate your love for me. Even at the moment the Angel Gabriel was announcing the good news to Mary, you were thinking about me and the joy your Son would bring to me, here and now, and later for all eternity. Thank you, Abba.

SECOND REFLECTION

v. 30 "Do not fear, Mary"

How often we find these words in Scripture. How often we need to hear: "Do not be afraid." Whenever we experience the presence and the power of God at work in our lives we are overwhelmed with awe and reverence. Our loving Father cautions us not to be afraid. How often Jesus tells us not to be afraid. Mary too was momentarily surprised by the "impossible" hence the angel bade her not to fear. When we realize that God loves us and permits nothing to happen to us which is not for our good, then we do not fear. As St. John assures us: "Love has no room for fear; rather, perfect love casts out all fear" *(I John 4:18).* Mary fearlessly accepted her role in God's plan of salvation. Daily Mary renewed her commitment without trepidation because she had experienced the Father's great love for her. Mary's love was so intense that she could give herself totally in return. (Rest in the Lord and let all fear drain from every part of your body.)

Colloquy: Mary, as my loving and solicitous Mother, teach me not to fear, but to step out in faith and always to say my yes to the Father without hesitation.

THIRD REFLECTION

v. 30 "You have found favor with God."

Our gracious Father called Mary to an extraordinary

role in the economy of salvation. Her special vocation was for the good of others, in fact for the salvation of the whole world. God calls each one of us to fulfill a certain role in life. It is often a ministry of service. God not only calls us, but he prepares us for that vocation by various steps throughout life. Finally he asks our commitment, just as he asks Mary for her *fiat*. We have found favor with God, now he is waiting for our response. (Reflect on your own commitment.)

Colloquy: Mary, teach me to listen so that I may hear God's call. Help me to submit to whatever conditioning God may ask and, like you, graciously and generously give myself to him.

FOURTH REFLECTION

v. 34 "How can this be since I do not know man?"

Even though Mary was asked to become involved in a phenomenon which had never taken place in the annals of human history, she did not dismiss the angel's announcement as ridiculous or impossible because she knew that God was at work. Mary's question was not so much one of doubt or hesitation. She did not ask for any explanations or guarantees. She asked only one question in order to ascertain God's will. With the assurance that this was what God was asking of her, she gave her unconditional acquiescence to the Lord. (Try to experience the Father's joy at Mary's unreserved gift of self.)

Colloquy: Jesus, like your Mother, your whole concern was doing the will of your Father. Help me to realize that only in doing what you ask of me, will I find peace and happiness in life.

FIFTH REFLECTION

v. 35 "The Holy Spirit will come upon you and the power of the Most High will overshadow you . . . ."

Mary is "our nature's solitary boast." Her sinlessness made her the temple of the Holy Spirit who was molding her precious soul into a vessel of election. Our loving Abba called us through our Baptism to become a member of his family. He adopted us as his sons and daughters. He comes to live within us by sharing his divine life with us. We, like Mary, become Christ-bearers as we permit his divine life and love to radiate through us to everyone we meet. This is our special apostolate. (Rest in God's abiding presence.)

Colloquy: Holy Spirit, keep me ever aware of how precious a temple I am. Empower me to become the apostle of love to which you have called me. I count on your divine influence to fulfill my role.

SIXTH REFLECTION

v. 36-37 "Know that Elizabeth, your kinswoman has conceived a son in her old age . . . for nothing is impossible with God."

God's plan unfolds in greater detail and in mysterious ways. The world must know that God's power was at work in the mystery of the Incarnation. John's birth was not to be an ordinary natural birth. God's power must be seen in Elizabeth's conception as foretold by the Angel to Zechariah. All must stand in awe, wonder and reverence as God's power is manifested. Likewise God's presence and power is manifested in every detail of our lives. We can recognize it only when we pause in prayer to listen. (Ponder his presence and power in your life.)

Colloquy: Father, I know you have plans for every detail of my life. How often I forget, yet how patiently you remind me from time to time when you permit the "extraordinary" to arrest my attention. Thank you for your patient endurance of my lack of faith.

v. 38 "I am the servant of the Lord. Let it be done to me as you say."

When a person experiences being loved so completely by God, he is incapable of being other than totally God's. Mary experienced being loved by God with a tender and total love. Her sinless soul made her more sensitive to the Father's love and also gave her a greater capacity to receive this infinite love. She could not be anything other than totally his. As we become more and more single-minded, our capacity to receive and experience the Father's love increases. Then we, like Mary, cannot help but respond in love and love means total giving of self. What peace and joy, what happiness and contentment, this commitment brings with it. (Bask in the sunshine of God's love.)

Colloquy: Mary, I too want to say: "I am the servant of the Lord. Let it be done to me as you say." Through your powerful intercession, please obtain that grace for me.

Additional suggested passages for prayer:

Hebrews 10:5-10	"I have come to do your will, O God."
John 1:11-18	"The Word became flesh. . . ."
	Kenosis:
Philippians 2:5-11	"He emptied himself. . . ."
Isaiah 7: 10-14	"The virgin shall be with child. . . ."
I Corinthians 1:25-31	"He singled out the weak of this world to shame the strong."

8 God Responds to Man's Need

He Made His Dwelling Among Us
Luke 2:1-20

An artist was once painting a picture of a wintry scene. He nestled a little cottage among large fir trees which were heavily laden with snow. The cottage too was covered with snow. It was a dark and dismal scene. It was without light and lonely. The artist studied the picture, stepped forward and with a few deft strokes of his brush, put light in the windows. Instantly the whole scene changed. Now it radiated charm and cheerfulness, comfort and coziness. Our world too was lightless and lonely. People lived with the promise that a redeemer would someday come. In God's own time, a light did come into our world. Jesus identified himself with that light: "I am the light of the world" *(John 8:12)*. Like the artist's painting the world began to change. Now there was hope and consolation, peace and joy because Jesus did come, not as a guest, but to stay, to live with us and within us. "The light shines on in darkness, a darkness that did not overcome it"

(John 1:5).

FIRST REFLECTION

v. 7 "She gave birth to her first-born son and wrapped him in swaddling clothes and laid him in a manger. . . ."
As we enter that humble hovel of a home and con-

template the infant wrapped in swaddling clothes and laying in a manger, we become lost in mystery. John summarizes this tremendous mystery of the Incarnation. Jesus became savior and Messiah because he loves us. "He emptied himself and took on the form of a slave being born in the likeness of men" because he loves us. (*Phil. 2:7*). He came that we "might have life and have it to the full" because he loves us. (*John 10:10*). Love is the only answer, the only explanation. (Let your heart pour out your love for him.)

Colloquy: Lord Jesus, how can I ever thank you for this great mystery of your incarnation into our sinful world? All I can do is offer you my love in return. Let me rest in your love.

SECOND REFLECTION

vv. 9-10 "You have nothing to fear!"

Whenever God manifests his presence and his power in our midst, there is always a caution not to be afraid. We find this consoling thought throughout all of the Scriptures. There are principally two kinds of fear. This requires some discernment. When fear arises from God's presence and power, there is always peace in our hearts. This kind of fear is mostly an awe and reverence for God. The second kind of fear is mostly worry, anxiety and distress which robs us of our peace. Obviously this fear is caused by the evil one who would wean us away from God. The angel assures the shepherds that they have come to proclaim the good news—tidings of great joy. We never tire of this story of God's love. Each time we hear the good news we stand in reverence and awe, as it fills us with peace and joy. (Rest in his presence and drink in the good news.)

Colloquy: Lord Jesus, thank you for the peace and joy which you bring to us each time we reflect on your great love for us. May I always radiate this peace and joy to all who cross my path.

THIRD REFLECTION

v. 11 "This day in David's city a savior has been born to
you, the Messiah and Lord."

In one brief sentence the angel revealed so much
about the person and office of Jesus. The angel called
him "savior" which recalls God's loving providence in
sending his Son to redeem us, to reunite us with him in
bonds of love after these bonds had been severed by
sin. Only God can save us. Jesus is called "Messiah";
God is faithful to his promises. For centuries Israel
lived with the hopeful and faithful expectation that
God would send them the Anointed One who would
redeem them. The angel calls Jesus "Lord". Yes, he is
Lord of all creation: "Through him all things came into
being" (*John 1:3*). He is a King who wants to establish a
spiritual kingdom of love. What profound mysteries
are contained in this brief announcement by the angels
to the shepherds! All this embodied in a helpless child!
That too is a mystery. (Rest with that mystery.)

Colloquy: My heart rejoices at your goodness to us in
giving us your only Son. Help me to enter more fully
into this great mystery so that I might respond with
greater love and dedication.

FOURTH REFLECTION

v. 14 "Glory to God in high heaven. . . ."

The joy of the Incarnation and the Nativity fills our
hearts so that we burst forth in songs of praise and
thanksgiving, just as the angels did when they appeared to the shepherds. In our lives we celebrate the
Nativity daily since Jesus is born again each day for us.
He is born again in his Word since each day we find
new inspiration and motivation for our personal journey to Emmaus. Each day Jesus comes to us to celebrate
the Eucharist so that we may have the nourishment to
continue faithfully our pilgrimage back to the Father.

Surely, he did not leave us orphans. How faithful he is to his promise: "Know that I am with you always, until the end of the world!" (*Matthew 28:20*). Little wonder that our hearts want to leap for joy as we sing "Glory to God in high heaven . . . ." (Be still and let the angelic chorus fill your heart.)

Colloquy: Jesus, you told us that you had come to fill us with joy so that your joy may be ours. Fill me with that deep down, quiet, interior joy so that I may radiate that joy, especially to those who do not know you.

FIFTH REFLECTION

v. 17 "Once they saw, they understood . . . ."

The shepherds believed and they trusted; hence "they went in haste and found Mary and Joseph and the baby lying in the manger." What an antithesis here! The angels called him Savior, Messiah, Lord, yet the shepherds saw only an impoverished, helpless child. Their faith was rewarded. Because they stepped out in faith and came in haste, they were gifted with an even greater faith: "Once they saw, they understood." God endowed them with this deeper faith. God's ways seem so strange to us. He wanted to reveal the good news to these simple men of the field because they would respond in faith. They would translate that faith into action and commitment. God further endowed them for "they understood" this great mystery of God's love. (Relax and let the Lord give you this gift too.)

Colloquy: Lord Jesus, there is so much I do not understand about you and your mysterious ways because I lack the faith of the simple shepherds. Please grant me the gift of a dynamic, operative faith of commitment and expectancy.

SIXTH REFLECTION

v. 19 "Mary treasured all these things and reflected on them in her heart."

The Gospel tells us so little about Mary. However, when she is mentioned, she is always such a beautiful model for us to follow. Mary is truly a contemplative. I am sure that Mary could not comprehend all the events which were happening in quick succession. She must have asked herself: "How could the shepherds know?" "How could they believe?" Mary turned to God in a loving prayer posture to let him teach her. She "treasured all these things and reflected on them." She had given herself totally to God. Now she tried to keep herself open and receptive to what God was doing in her and through her. Prayer is a lifestyle. Prayer is living in union with God. Prayer requires time to be quiet and ponder God's mysterious ways. Prayer means to be an open vessel so that God might fill us with his divine life and love. Prayer means loving God. All this Mary teaches us by her whole lifestyle, especially at this peak moment in salvation history. (Be for God and let him be for you.)

Colloquy: Mary, as my loving Mother, teach me to pray, teach me to rest in God's presence. Lead me to your Son Jesus so that I may live, move and be with him and for him alone.

SEVENTH REFLECTION

v. 20 "The shepherds returned, glorifying and praising God for all they had heard and seen. . . ."

The shepherds had experienced the presence and the power of God in their lives. Now their hearts were filled with joy and thanksgiving. They praised and glorified God for all his goodness to them and to the "whole people." To praise and glorify God is one of the highest forms of prayer. God wants our praise. Through the psalmist he tells us: "He that offers praise as a sacrifice glorifies me" (Psalm 50:23). The prophet assures us that God lives in the praises of his people. Each Christmas we pause to celebrate and be joyous as we recall once again the Father's goodness to us. It is a time of gift-giving. We give gifts to one another as we remember the greatest of all God's gifts to us, his own divine Son. (Let your heart pour out its praise to God.)

Colloquy: God our Father, you gave us the greatest of all your gifts, your own divine Son. All you ask of me is the gift of myself in return. That is difficult at times. With your help may I graciously and generously say yes to you each day.

The following Scripture passages may help us to pray with the same theme:

John 1:1-18	"The Word became flesh and made his dwelling among us. . . ."
Matthew 1:18-25	"And they shall call him Emmanuel. . . God is with us. . . ."
Isaiah 9:1-7	"A child is born to us, a son is given us. . . ."
Titus 2:11-14	"The grace of God has appeared, offering salvation to all men. . . ."
Titus 3:3-7	"When the kindness and love of God our savior appeared. . . ."

9 Baptism of Jesus

Jesus Coming From Galilee, Appeared Before John
Matthew 3:11-17

Accompany Jesus as he leaves his home town of Nazareth and wends his way toward the Jordan River where John was baptizing. What thoughts must have filled his mind now that he was about to begin his public ministry! Was his heart heavy at leaving his Mother, his home, his familiar haunts as a child? Did his ministry loom up in his mind as an impossible task? Did he pray that he might be able to touch the hearts of the people he loved? Was he concerned about the humiliation of being associated with sinners in the rite of baptism?

Walk along with Jesus in silence. Let your heart listen to his silence.

FIRST REFLECTION

v. 11 "He it is who will baptize you in the Holy Spirit and fire."

Jesus instituted a sacramental rite so that we could be baptized with the Holy Spirit and fire. He explains to us how important Baptism is: "No one can enter into God's kingdom without being begotten of water and Spirit" (*John* 3:5). The day of our Baptism is the most important day of our lives here in this land of exile. In Baptism God invites us to become members of his family; we become his adopted sons and daughters.

God is our Father; we belong to him. Our loving Father also shares with us at that time the greatest of all his gifts, his own divine life. Jesus came into the world to make this incorporation possible through his death and resurrection. The Holy Spirit completes this work within us through this sacramental rite. (Let this truth take possession of you.)

Colloquy: Father, I want to spend this day in a special way thanking you for inviting me and accepting me into your family. Teach me what a great dignity is mine and also help me to recognize the dignity of my brothers and sisters who are also your adopted sons and daughters.

SECOND REFLECTION

v. 12 "He will clear the threshing floor. . . ."

John the Baptizer came to prepare the way for the coming of Jesus. He was calling all men to repentance in preparation for the coming of the Messiah. John tells us that we must make a choice either to accept Jesus in faith and turn away from sin or disregard the invitation of Jesus to become one of his followers. Jesus could spell it out plainly: "He who is not with me is against me." Jesus came to call all men to salvation including you and me. However, he is a gentle, sensitive God and will not force us. He invites us to his way of life hoping that we will love enough to accept his invitation. On the other hand even if we disregard his invitation, he will continue to seek us out, always respecting our free will which tragically permits us to say no to love. Jesus explains this truth so graphically in the story of the Last Judgment (*Matthew 25:31-46*). (Listen to Jesus inviting you.)

Colloquy: Jesus, I want to commit myself totally to you so that when your winnowing fan has done its work, I may remain as grain to be gathered into your barn. Grant me the gift of always saying yes to you.

THIRD REFLECTION

v. 13 "Jesus . . . appeared before John at the Jordan to
    be baptized by him."

A great moment in salvation history had arrived.
Jesus was about to begin his public ministry. He inau-
gurated his mission with a tremendous act of humility.
He, whose divine nature is diametrically opposed to
sin, took his place among sinners to submit to this
ritual "for the sake of reform." As Paul could say: "He
emptied himself and took the form of a slave, being
born in the likeness of men" (*Philippians 2:7*). Jesus, the
transcendent God of heaven and earth, humbly submitted to one of his creatures. What a condescension!
Jesus had taken upon himself the burden of our sins;
therefore, he submitted, as a common sinner, to this
purifying ceremony. (Sit on Jordan's bank and try to
grasp what is taking place.)

Colloquy: Lord Jesus, I lay all my faults and failures,
my sins and shortcomings at your feet. Help me to
realize that you are more eager to forgive and to heal
than I am to be forgiven. That is the mystery of your
love. Thank you for this example of humility.

FOURTH REFLECTION

v. 14 "I should be baptized by you, yet you come to
    me!"

Jesus came to the Jordan to sanctify John's mission.
He also drew near to sanctify John the Baptizer. He
came to drown our sinfulness in the waters of the
Jordan. Jesus sanctified "the waters of the Jordan"
which is our baptismal water and which signifies the
outpouring of the Holy Spirit upon each one of us in
Baptism. As Paul reminds us: "If we have been united
with him through likeness to his death, so shall we be
through a like resurrection" (*Romans 6:3-11*). (Feel the
cleansing waters of Baptism purifying you.)

Colloquy: Jesus, let me go down with you as you were

being baptized so that I may rise with you bathed in the light of your glory. Thank you for calling me to my own Baptism.

FIFTH REFLECTION

v. 15 "We must do this if we would fulfill all of God's demands. . . ."

Jesus was always deeply concerned about doing the will of his Father. He fulfilled his Father's commands to the very letter. He went even further. He was most solicitous about obeying even the slightest wish of his Father: "Let it be as you would have it, not as I." Jesus went to the extreme. He had experienced the infinite love of the Father for him, and he also loved us with an infinite love, hence he could give nothing less than the total and complete gift of himself as he did on Calvary. Since he poured out every last drop of blood and water, there was nothing more to give. That's how complete his total response in love was. (Let the words of Jesus touch your soul.)

Colloquy: Jesus, my greatest treasure is my own will, my own plans, my own ambitions. How difficult it is for me to submit totally to your will, yet I know that only in your will will I find true peace. Help me to want to respond to the Father's will with the same generosity and love with which you responded.

SIXTH REFLECTION

v. 16 "He saw the Spirit of God descend like a dove and hover over him."

The appearance of the Spirit of God in the form of a dove brings us to an awareness of the awesome mystery of the blessed Trinity which was gradually being revealed to us. The Spirit of God appeared in visible form not only to reveal himself as the third person of the blessed Trinity, but also to distinguish the Baptism which Jesus was to institute from that of John. "I baptize you in water . . . He will baptize you in the Holy Spirit and fire." The Holy Spirit is the source of divine life and love. In Baptism he comes to dwell "with" us and "within" us, thus making our bodies his temple. (Experience the presence and power of the Holy Spirit within you.)

Colloquy: O Holy Spirit dwelling within me as your temple, you are purifying and sanctifying me by your very presence. Let me express my gratitude by striving to be receptive to your presence and power within me and to respond graciously and generously to your inspirations and guidance. "Here I am, Lord."

SEVENTH REFLECTION

v. 17 "This is my beloved Son. My favor rests on him."

The Father knows how weak and wavering our faith can be. In these words he himself confirms the mission of Jesus. He did so twice during Jesus' earthly sojourn. At the time of the Baptism of Jesus, the Father confirmed the teaching mission of Jesus. As this mission was drawing to a close, the Father confirmed Jesus' ministry of suffering. He did so at the Transfiguration on Mount Tabor. "This is my Son, my Chosen One. Listen to him." How gracious of the Father to condescend to our human weakness. He knew how hard it would be for us to grasp the dreadful sufferings, the apparent defeat, which Jesus had to endure. He gives us the assurance that this is all in his salvific plan. (Let the Father's words rest in your heart.)

Colloquy: Father, I beg you to give me a strong, dynamic faith, which will readily help me to recognize and be receptive to all your communications. Father, with Peter I say: "How good it is for us to be here."

To continue your prayer with this mystery of God's love, we suggest the following passages:

John 3:1-21   "No one can enter into God's kingdom without being begotten of water and Spirit."

Romans 6:1-23   "Are you not aware that we who
                   were baptized into Christ Jesus
                   were baptized into his death?"

Matthew 28:18-20   "Baptize them in the name of the
                   Father, . . ."

10 Temptation in the Desert

Relive With Jesus His Desert Experience
Matthew 4:1-11

Jesus teaches us many valuable lessons from his own desert experience. He points out to us how cunning and deceptive are the wiles of Satan. He shows us how much we need the gifts of grace and discernment. He teaches us to be singleminded in doing God's will regardless of the enticements and clever machinations of the devil. Jesus invites us now, in prayer, to relive these experiences with him as our Risen Lord, so that we may find hope and encouragement for the encounters which we will inevitably experience along the highway of life.

FIRST REFLECTION

v. 1 "Then Jesus was led into the desert by the Spirit to be tempted by the devil."

God can often be found more easily in the desert. With large expanses of bleak rock and dry sand, with little or no sign of life, our attention naturally turns toward God and rivets itself on him alone. Since it is impossible to exist in some desert areas without the loving, providential care of God, a desert experience can aid us in sorting out the proper priorities in life. Israel experienced this total and complete dependence on God in the Sinai desert. They had no food, no water. God provided the manna, the quail and the springs of fresh water. He did even more. Their clothes did not wear out, nor were they weary or footsore from walking. They recognized their total dependence on God. We too must find God in the desert. It may be a geographic desert, a hermitage, a place apart. More frequently it means solitude in our own heart. We need to take time from the feverish activity of every day to be alone with God. At the core of silence and solitude we find him. In the desert our mundane and myopic view becomes more cosmic and transcendent. (Rest in solitude.)

Colloquy: Father, thank you for inviting me to come apart into a desert place to sort out my priorities. Help me keep my focus ever on you so that I may walk in your presence always.

SECOND REFLECTION

v. 2 "He fasted forty days and forty nights, and afterward was hungry."

Jesus taught us the value and proper use of many things in our lives. He pointed out how frequently fasting is recommended in the Scriptures. Now Jesus teaches us by his own example. Fasting is not primarily a mortification, but rather a discipline to assist us in raising our focus above the mundane to the celestial. Fasting helps us change our attitudes. It helps us avoid self-centeredness and self-indulgence. Fasting helps us enter into a deeper prayer posture. When we fast, according to our own ability, God becomes more real to us. It is easier for us to reach out to him. He is more present to us. Prayer comes more readily. When we try to come closer to our loving Father by prayer and fasting, the evil one will use all his wiles to wean us away from God or to discourage us in our efforts to deepen our relationship with our loving Abba. Jesus prepared us for this by his own example in thwarting the devil's attempts. (Be with Jesus in the desert.)

Colloquy: Father, how often you invite me to fast, yet how reluctant I am to respond to your invitation. Jesus, on one occasion you told us that we could break the influence of the evil one only by prayer and fasting. In moments of temptation teach me to pray and fast.

THIRD REFLECTION

v. 3 "The tempter approached and said to him, . . ."

The temptations of Jesus in the desert have a threefold significance. 1) They recall all the temptations which the Israelites endured in the desert of Sinai. Unfortunately the Israelites failed the test. 2) The temptations which beset Jesus were those he faced throughout his whole earthly sojourn. Unlike the Israelites of old, Jesus annihilated the cunning of the evil one. 3) These temptations summarize all the temptations which beseige us during our life on earth. How often the devil appeals to our pride, our self-will, our desire for power and prestige. In reality the devil was suggesting to Jesus that he accomplish his mission in an easier way. Jesus was able to conquer these temptations because he had come to do the will of the Father. He was singleminded in this: "I have come to do your will, O God." Nothing was going to deter him. Jesus invites us to live these experiences with him so that we may find hope, courage and reassurance in our daily struggle. He reminds us that we are not alone. He is always with us. (Be alone in the desert.)

Colloquy: Jesus, grant me the humility to recognize that by myself, I cannot survive. Keep reminding me of your words: "Apart from me, you can do nothing" and "My grace is enough for you."

FOURTH REFLECTION

v. 3 "If you are the Son of God, command these stones to turn into bread."

When we strive to live a deeper union with our

loving Father, the devil works more vigorously to wean us away from our purpose. At such times, he does not usually entice us with an invitation to grave sin. More frequently he tries to divert our resolution with fears, doubts and misgivings. He strikes at our weakest point, our Achilles' heel. He did the same with Jesus. Jesus was hungry. The devil urged him to satisfy his hunger in such a way that people would flock to him in wonderment. Thus he could more easily establish his kingdom. How frequently the devil holds up to us an apparent good to lead us away from God. He is subtle, but not very powerful. The devil has no sense of humor; therefore laugh at him and at yourself. It will confound him. (Enjoy the Peace of Jesus.)

Colloquy: Holy Spirit, endow me with your special gifts of wisdom, understanding, prudence and discernment so that I may see clearly the wiles of the evil one in my daily living. Grant me the strength to turn away from his enticements without hesitation.

FIFTH REFLECTION

v. 4 "Not on bread alone is man to live but on every utterance that comes from the mouth of God."

Jesus suffered the same temptations which Israel faced in the desert. Notice the symbolism in the forty years' wandering and the forty days' fast of Jesus in the desert. Israel rebelled against God because they had no food. They longed for the fleshpots of Egypt. In spite of their murmuring against God, our provident Father supplied all their needs, not only food and water for their physical needs, but his Word and promises for their spiritual needs. He revealed himself and his law to them. He gave them the assurance that if they accepted his Law, they would be his people and he would be their God. The decalogue which he gave them on Mount Sinai welded them into a people to be respected, a community set apart. He did this in spite of their rebellion. God does the same for us. He has given us his Word as well as his divine life in the Eucharist. We are his people. (Soak in the presence of Jesus.)

Colloquy: Father, how easily I forget. Thank you for nourishing me with your Word. When I become anxious and unduly concerned about the temporalities of life, remind me that I am to live on every utterance that comes from your mouth. Thank you for your patience with me.

SIXTH REFLECTION

v. 5-7 "If you are the Son of God, throw yourself down. . . ."

In this temptation the evil one was encouraging Jesus to use his divine power to produce a spectacular display and thus convince the people that he is God. Such an event, the devil argued, would cause many people to believe in him. The devil himself was trying to determine whether or not Jesus was really God. Jesus remained singleminded. He had come to do the will of the Father and nothing was going to deter him from it. In effect the devil was asking Jesus to do it the easy way. Jesus did not yield. He was adamant. Jesus acted against the temptation using the same tactics which the evil one used. The devil quoted Scripture to convince Jesus. In turn Jesus quoted the words of his Father: "You shall not put the Lord your God to the test." (In solitude adore Jesus living within you.)

Colloquy: Father, how often I question your way of doing things! How often I put you to the test! How pelagian I am! Let me become more like Jesus who was always a "yes" to you.

SEVENTH REFLECTION

vv. 8-11 "All these will I bestow on you if you prostrate yourself in homage before me. . . ."

In this temptation, the devil was trying to persuade

Jesus to use political power and influence to establish his kingdom. How deceptive is the evil one. He is a liar from the beginning. He had no power to give away "all the kingdoms of the world." How often the devil appeals to us in the same way! How frequently he holds up worldly "success" as the ultimate achievement in life. How easily the false gods of wealth, power, prestige, pleasure and our need for acceptance creep into our lives without our being aware of them. How like the rich young man we are! (*Mark 10:17ff*). Jesus' response was severe and final: "Away with you, Satan!" How beautifully Jesus reminded us of the proper priorities in our own lives when he said: "You shall do homage to the Lord your God; him alone shall you adore." (Let the words of Jesus find a home in your heart.)

Colloquy: Lord Jesus, thank you for the powerful example you gave me in this episode. Pour your Spirit upon me so that I can truly discern the tactics of the evil one in my daily living. Be with me always to strengthen my weak will.

To continue your contemplative prayer with Jesus at the time of his temptation we recommend the following texts:

I Corinthians 10:1-13	"He will not let you be tested beyond your strength."
James 1:12-15	"Happy the man who holds out to the end through trial!"
Luke 4:1-14	Temptation in the Desert
Mark 1:12-13	Temptation of Jesus

11 The Beatitudes

What Was Jesus Like?
Matthew 5:3-12

How much we would like to know what Jesus looked like! Was he tall or short in stature, slightly built or stocky, light or dark in complexion? We have no physical picture of Jesus, not even a verbal delineation of his features. However, in the Gospel Jesus did reveal much about himself, his personality and his character. In teaching us the Beatitudes, which are the Magna Carta of Christianity, Jesus was really saying: "This is what I am, this is what I stand for, this is my way of life." As we listen prayerfully to these teachings of Jesus, his personality unfolds for us and impresses itself deeply on our hearts. Even though we may not be consciously aware of it, as we listen to his Words our thoughts and attitudes will be conforming to those of Jesus. We will be identifying with him.

FIRST REFLECTION

v. 3 "How blest are the poor in spirit: the reign of God is theirs."

Jesus was poor in spirit. He came to do the will of the Father. He manifested his complete dependence on his Father. Jesus told us: "Apart from me you can do nothing." How true! When we recognize our total dependence on God, we are poor in spirit. After all, what can we do by ourselves? Nothing, really, for even our next heartbeat is God's gift to us. This total dependence is not a sign of weakness, but merely the recognition of God as our loving, provident, compassionate Abba. (Sit quietly in his presence.)

Colloquy: Jesus, you are saying to me that when I strive to become poor in spirit, I am identifying more closely with you, and that I will be blessed with that peace, serenity, tranquillity and joy which the world cannot give. I will become more like you.

SECOND REFLECTION

v. 4 "Blest too are the sorrowing; they shall be consoled."

Too often we look upon human affliction and sorrow as a punishment for sin. Jesus told us that our sorrow would be turned into joy, because suffering is frequently the road to real joy and happiness. Jesus was sorrowful as he wept over the city of Jerusalem, as he watched his disciples leaving him when he promised them himself in the Eucharist and when he faced death. Jesus always reached out to the suffering. He healed, he comforted, he fed them. He brought them hope and promise, peace and joy. (Enjoy the comfort of his presence.)

Colloquy: Jesus, I too must reach out to all the suffering if I am to identify with you and be your disciple. Keep me open and receptive so that you may reach out through me to all those suffering in any way. Thus I can become the channel of your love to them.

THIRD REFLECTION

v. 6 "Blest are they who hunger and thirst for holiness; they shall have their fill."

The very desire to establish a deeper relationship with God is a gift from the Holy Spirit. If we use that gift well, we shall certainly be blessed. We use God's gift well by spending time in prayerful listening, by striving for an openness to what God wants to effect in us. This will mean giving up our own will at times. It means becoming more indifferent to our pet projects and programs. It means that our loving Father and his Son Jesus will become the number-one-priority of our lives so that we can form a deeper, richer relationship with Jesus. (Listen to your own heart's desire.)

Colloquy: Holy Spirit, I thank you for endowing me with a hunger and thirst for a more personal union with Jesus. Give me the grace to respond generously and graciously to your "gifted" invitation.

FOURTH REFLECTION

v. 7 "Blest are they who show mercy; mercy shall be theirs."

The whole public life of Jesus was a ministry of mercy and compassion. No suffering escaped his notice, nor his healing power. He showed great compassion for the widow of Naim, the blind Bartimaeus, the ten lepers—to mention only a few occasions. Jesus reached out with loving mercy to the sinful woman in Simon's house, to the woman taken in adultery, to the Good Thief on the cross. Even in his darkest hour he only pleaded for mercy, but he excused his enemies when he prayed: "Father, forgive them; they do not know what they are doing" (*Luke 23:34*). If we are to be his disciples we, like him, must radiate mercy and compassion at all times. (Be still. Let him fill you with his mercy.)

Colloquy: Jesus, you bade us: "Be compassionate, as your Father is compassionate" (*Luke 6:36*).

As I reflect on your compassion, help me rid myself of any self-centeredness which would prevent me from reaching out in loving compassion as you did.

FIFTH REFLECTION

v. 8 "Blest are the single-hearted for they shall see God."

It was written of Jesus long before he was incarnated in our world that he was coming to do the will of his Father. "As is written of me in the book, I have come to do your will, O God" (*Hebrews 10:7*). Again Jesus said: "The world must know that I love the Father and do as the Father has commanded me" (*John 14:31*). Even in that dreadful agony in the Garden of Gethsemane, Jesus had only one purpose: to do what the Father asked of him: "My Father, if it is possible, let this cup pass me by. Still, let it be as you would have it, not as I" (*Matthew 26:39*). (Listen to Jesus' yes to his Father.)

SIXTH REFLECTION

v. 9 "Blest too the peacemakers; they shall be called sons of God."

The night before he died Jesus promised us his peace. "Peace is my farewell to you, my peace is my gift to you." After his Resurrection his constant greeting was "Peace be with you." The peace which Jesus came to give is the fruit of his divine life dwelling within us. Peace is one of the fruits of the Holy Spirit abiding within us for we are his temple. Like love, peace isn't peace until we have given it away. Jesus infuses us with his peace each day at the Eucharistic Celebration. At the close of that Celebration he invites us to become a channel of his peace to others. This is our apostolate. (Let peace permeate you thoroughly.)

Colloquy: Jesus, the evil one is determined to destroy your gift of peace within me so that I cannot be at peace myself nor bring your peace to others. Break his bonds, give me the insight to discern his deceits and above all make me a channel of your *peace*.

SEVENTH REFLECTION

vv. 10-12 "Blest are those persecuted for holiness' sake. . . ."

The whole life of Jesus was one of rejection—from

the time of his birth until that rejection which culminated in his death. Furthermore, Jesus warned us that if they persecuted him, they will also persecute us, his followers. The standards of the world are diametrically opposed to the objectives which Jesus set up in his kingdom. We must constantly remind ourselves of this truth, because by our very nature we want to be accepted by others. St. Paul tells us "We are fools on Christ's account." Jesus himself prepared us for the attitude of the world: "If you find that the world hates you know it hated me before you . . . the reason it hates you is that you do not belong to the world. But I chose you out of the world" (*John 15:18ff*). ("Be glad and rejoice.")

Colloquy: Jesus, when I get to know how precious your love is for me, the hatred of the world becomes unimportant. Keep my gaze riveted on your love, then I will welcome persecution as you did, then I can "be glad and rejoice."

To discover more about what Jesus was like, we suggest praying with the following passages:

John 14:6-7	"I am the way, and the truth, and the life. . . ."
Mark 8:31-38	"You are not judging by God's standards but by man's."
James 4:1-10	"Are you not aware that love of the world is enmity to God?"
John 9:5	"I am the light of the world."
Mark 14:60-65	"Are you the Messiah? . . . ."
Luke 2:11	"This day in David's city a savior has been born to you, the Messiah and Lord."

12 Come Follow Me

The Call, Conditioning, And Commitment To Discipleship
Luke 9:57-62

If we were commissioned to announce the coming of Jesus into the world and the advent of the whole Christian era, I wonder how we might begin. Surely we would inform the news media to assure television, radio and newspaper coverage. Perhaps we would reserve the largest superdome we could find to gather tens of thousands of people together for the event. Thus our plans would evolve in gigantic proportions. God's ways are not our ways, however. How differently Jesus announced the coming of the kingdom. He appeared among sinners and submitted to the baptismal ceremony "for the sake of reform." Unceremoniously he invited two would-be disciples to "Come, and see." He continued his invitation "Come, follow me" and "Come after me." This was his simple invitation without any promises of power, prestige, or possessions, only persecution.

Jesus proffers that same invitation to us today. He invites us into discipleship so that we can reach our eternal destiny and so that we may also be the channels whereby the good news may reach others. What a privilege to receive a personal invitation from Jesus himself!

FIRST REFLECTION

v. 57 "I will be your follower wherever you go."

Jesus had a tremendously magnetic personality. He radiated love, peace and joy at all times. We are naturally attracted to what is good and beautiful; hence this disciple wanted to follow Jesus wherever he went. The teachings of Jesus held out hope and promise to him. He must have been deeply impressed by Jesus' attitude toward the poor and the downtrodden. The healing power of Jesus made a deep impression upon him also. Above all the loving concern of Jesus for everyone must have been the deciding factor in his resolve to follow Jesus. Deep in the heart of this disciple there was a longing for all that Jesus stood for. Jesus too must have been pleased at his response and his desire to become his disciple. (Be alone with Jesus.)

Colloquy: Jesus, you place every wholesome desire and wish in our hearts. Please continue to fill my heart with the longing to follow you and be with you always and everywhere.

SECOND REFLECTION

v. 58 "The foxes have lairs, the birds of the sky have nests, but the Son of Man has nowhere to lay his head."

Jesus did not want to trick anyone into becoming his disciple. He was very honest and forthright with this man. Jesus could offer him no material gain, no rewards for service. Jesus was poor and wanted this prospective disciple to recognize his poverty. This meant quite a renunciation for this man, since among the Jews poverty was considered a punishment from God. According to their thinking, if a man lived a good life, God would reward him with good health and considerable wealth. Jesus cannot offer any material gain, but he can give us a peace, joy and happiness which the world cannot give. That joy and satisfaction is far beyond what money can buy. (Let Jesus speak to your heart.)

Colloquy: Jesus, how can I thank you for calling me to be your disciple? You cannot offer us any material gain, but you do give us the gift of yourself. What greater gain can there be!

THIRD REFLECTION

v. 59 "Come after me."

What a simple, but direct invitation from Jesus! "Come after me." He invites us in the same way to become his disiciples. There are three stages in discipleship. The first is the CALL. Jesus invites us to follow him. As Jesus tells us: "It was not you who chose me, it was I who chose you" (*John 15:16*). Our vocation is a gift from God. He places a desire, a longing within our hearts to want to come and follow him. God loves us so much that he gives us the impression that he needs us. He loves us so much that he wants us to be closely united with him. Jesus calls us not only to follow in his footsteps, but to be closely identified with him in our thinking, our attitudes, our mentality. (Listen to Jesus say to you: "Come after me.")

Colloquy: Lord Jesus, how can I ever thank you for inviting me to become one of your disciples? What trust and confidence you must have in me! Only with your help can I respond to your call. Grant me that grace.

FOURTH REFLECTION

v. 59 "Let me bury my father first."

Jesus must have been pleased with the filial piety of this man who wanted to care for his father and family before giving up everything to follow him. However, Jesus was trying to impress on him that the time is now. Renunciation of family is just another condition for the radical following of Jesus. Jesus also knew that family obligations will never cease. There will always be some need for a disciple to remain with his family to care for them. Thus he would never be able to follow his call. Jesus gave us an example himself. He left his Mother, who apparently had no one to care for her. He left his home town of Nazareth where he felt comfortable with his family and friends. (Reflect on your daily response to Jesus.)

Colloquy: Jesus, I can become so easily attached to family and friends and become so involved that I do not hear your call. Fill me with a great love and longing to respond to your invitation so that no attachment will impede my coming to you.

FIFTH REFLECTION

v. 60 "Let the dead bury their dead; come away and proclaim the kingdom of God."

This statement may seem rather harsh, coming from Jesus, until we understand that he did not mean it literally. Jesus was saying that those spiritually dead, those not interested in his kingdom, could bury those physically dead. Jesus wanted to impress upon his hearers how total their commitment to him must be and their dedication to the kingdom. A disciple is more than a student who attends lectures. A disciple follows his master by living with him. He strives to captivate the mentality, the attitudes, the personality of the master. A disciple learns by watching his master deal with various situations in life. It is an internship, an on-the-job training in the strictest sense of the term. Jesus calls us to be with him at all times, at work, at home, at play. (Rest in Jesus' presence and let your heart beat in tune with his.)

Colloquy: Jesus, you advised us to learn from you because you are gentle and humble of heart. Keep me aware that you are with me and within me at all times so that I may follow so closely in your footsteps that I can be identified with you.

SIXTH REFLECTION

v. 61 "I will be your follower, Lord, but first let me take leave of my people at home."

The second step toward discipleship is A CONVERSION or CONDITIONING. When Jesus calls us to discipleship, he knows that we are often self-centered. He lays down some conditions for his followers. Jesus told us that his disciples would have to "take up his cross each day, and follow in my steps" (*Luke 9:23*). He told the rich man: "Go and sell what you have and give to the poor" (*Mark 10:21*). Another requirement for discipleship was to be willing to die to self. Listen to his words: "Unless the grain of wheat falls to the earth and dies, it remains just a grain of wheat . . . ." (*John 12:24*). Jesus was pointing out to us how complete, how radical, how total our commitment must be. It may require considerable conditioning before we are able to make a commitment as unqualified as Mary's *fiat*. (Be assured that as soon as the words of Jesus touch your heart, they are already conditioning you.)

Colloquy: Jesus, let me walk with you, let me come to know you better each day so that I may acquire a fresh spiritual way of thinking and put on the new man. Only when my attitude is the same as yours can I be your disciple. I want to be your disciple. I beg you to accept me. Help me to submit to your conditioning.

SEVENTH REFLECTION

v. 62 "Whoever puts his hand to the plow but keeps looking back is unfit for the reign of God."

The third step in discipleship is COMMITMENT. Commitment means the gift of ourselves. It is an ongoing giving of self and must be continually renewed. This is what Jesus meant when he said: "Whoever puts his hand to the plow but keeps looking back is unfit for the reign of God." Jesus was assuring us that we will never reach a point where we might rest on our laurels and simply enjoy our accomplishments. We must continue to renew our commitment as our mission in life continues to unfold each day. Such a total commitment can be made only if we love. When we experience God's infinite love for us, we cannot help but give ourselves completely to him. For the person who has experienced God's love no words are necessary. For the person who does not know God's love, no words can explain it for him. (Be still and let God love you.)

Colloquy: Jesus, you were singleminded in doing your Father's will. There was never any question or hesitation in your mind. Fill me with your love so that I too may commit myself graciously and generously and without hesitation.

To pursue this theme in your prayer, we suggest the following texts:

John 1:35-51	"Come and see . . . ."
Luke 9:23-27	". . . take up his cross each day. . . ."
Matthew 20:24-28	"Here we have put everything aside to follow you. . . ."
John 13:12-17	"Do you understand what I just did for you?"
Matthew 14:1-21	Herod's Banquet and Jesus' Banquet

13 Jesus Meets A Samaritan Woman At Jacob's Well

Called To Be An Apostle of Love
John 4:4-42

In this encounter of Jesus with the Samaritan woman at Jacob's well, we discover Jesus as a person of great kindness and understanding. As we listen with our whole being to the Word of God, we begin to read between the lines. It is like receiving a letter from a loved one. As we read the letter, we not only recognize the voice of the person speaking, but we are also aware of much which is not said. Likewise as we pray with Sacred Scripture, we begin to hear many nuances and overtones which tell us what Jesus was like. We begin to know Jesus better, not only by what he says, but also by what he does. Take your place at Jacob's well and listen with your heart and let your heart speak to Jesus. He hears the prayers of the heart more readily than those that are only of the lips.

FIRST REFLECTION

vv. 4-9 "Give me a drink."

Jesus revealed much about himself by the sensitivity and delicacy of his approach to the Samaritan woman. The Jews were by no means friendly to the Samaritans, nor was this much-married woman socially acceptable to her own people. This is probably why she came out to the well at high noon, instead of joining the rest of the women in their daily trek to the well. Jesus gently reached out in love to her. He asked a favor from her rather than impose himself upon her. She was naturally startled because Jews would not even use a vessel once a Samaritan had taken food or drink from it. She was startled and asked, "You are a Jew. How can you ask me, a Samaritan and a woman, for a drink?" How gracious and gentle is Jesus! How much he reveals about himself as we become present in this encounter. (Rest at the well with Jesus.)

Colloquy: Jesus, as a teacher, you are the greatest. You bade me come to learn from you for you are gentle and humble of heart. Be with me in prayer and teach my heart to radiate your gentleness and humility.

SECOND REFLECTION

vv. 10-15 "If only you recognized God's gift . . . he would have given you living water."

Jesus explains the tremendous mystery of his divine life and his indwelling with an appropriate symbol—living water. Water, so essential to life, is such an apt symbol of his divine life dwelling within each one of us. Jesus came into the world not only to die for our sins, but to share his divine life with us. At Baptism we are made the adopted sons and daughters of God; we become members of God's family. God grants us the greatest possible gift—a sharing in his divine life. That is what makes us a Christian—his indwelling. Jesus points out that he alone can satisfy the restless hunger and thirst within us: "Whoever drinks the water I give him will never be thirsty." Gradually and gently Jesus led the Samaritan woman to appreciate the living water of his divine life. If we are willing to set down our water pot and listen, Jesus will do the same for us who are so engrossed in the temporalities of each day. (Let his living water flood your whole being.)

Colloquy: Jesus, you promised that you would make your dwelling in me if I love you. You know how much

I want to love you. Give me the desire to want to love you more and more each day.

THIRD REFLECTION

vv. 16-18 "Go, call your husband. . . ."

How gently Jesus led the Samaritan woman into seeing herself as she appeared before God. Jesus did not condemn, nor threaten, nor did he condone her much-married state. He did touch a vulnerable area because he was trying to initiate a conversion process within her. This poor woman must have felt rejection from her fellow villagers. Perhaps that is why she came to the well all alone at high noon. Every disciple is first called, then conditioned and converted, before being asked to commit himself totally. This woman was experiencing a conversion. When we step into the sunshine of his divine presence, we see ourselves more clearly. When we pray his Word, when we expose our thoughts and feelings to that Word, we more readily recognize the areas and attitudes which are not totally in conformity with the mentality of Jesus. His Word has a powerful, purifying effect on us. Did Jesus not say: "You are clean already, thanks to the word I have spoken to you" (*John 15:3*). (Be still and experience his love.)

Colloquy: Jesus, as I pray with your Word, help me to see my own reflection. Show me those areas where I am not the kind of person you want me to be. Grant me the courage to conform more fully to the ideal you set for me.

FOURTH REFLECTION

vv. 19-26 "I know there is a Messiah coming . . . I who speak to you am he."

The Samaritan woman was moving toward faith. She was open and receptive to the influence of God's grace. As Jesus reached out in love to this poor woman, she recognized him as a prophet: "I can see you are a prophet." She was struggling with her faith. She did not know whether the Jews or her own people were correct in where and how God wanted to be worshipped. Jesus then revealed himself as he never did before and only once afterward. He admitted that he was the Messiah. "I who speak to you am he." This should be a great source of hope and encouragement to us. In spite of our frailty, our weak faith, our lack of generous response to his love, Jesus continues to bless us. It does not depend so much on our efforts as on the outpouring of his great love for us. (Spend some time in his presence.)

Colloquy: Lord, continue to reveal yourself to me as you did to the Samaritan woman. I need to be experientially aware of your presence and your love if I am to be your disciple and your apostle. Grant me that gift.

FIFTH REFLECTION

vv. 27-30 "The woman then left her water jar and went off into the town."

All prayer must be permeated with a spirit of gratitude. We cannot be prayerful persons unless we are grateful persons. Thanksgiving always characterized the prayer of Jesus. He was continually thanking his Father. The Samaritan woman teaches us a valuable lesson. She was so grateful to Jesus that she left her water jar for Jesus and his disciples, who had returned at this point, to quench their thirst. She shared her gift of water even though it might not yet have been living water. We can also show gratitude by using well the gift that has been given us. The Samaritan woman did just that. She began immediately to invite her own people to "Come and see someone who told me everything I ever did!" She began her apostolate by bringing others to Jesus. (Give the gift of yourself to Jesus.)

Colloquy: O gracious Father, how thoughtless I am!

94

How frequently I take your gifts for granted. Grant me the grace to pause each day to reflect on your countless gifts and also to say thank you from the depths of my being. May I never be counted among the other nine.

SIXTH REFLECTION

vv. 31-38 "Doing the will of him who sent me and bringing his work to completion is my food. . . ."

Jesus was singleminded in his mission on earth. He had come to bring the good news and nothing could interfere with that work. This was the will of the Father. Jesus also reveals the longing of his heart. He wants everyone to hear the good news and to accept him. Yes, "the fields are shining for harvest!" Jesus was pleading for laborers in his harvest. He wants disciples who will bring the good news of salvation not only by word but by the example of their own lives. As Jesus calls us into a deeper commitment as disciples, he reminds us: "The gift you have received, give as a gift" (*Mt. 10:8*). Our Christian heritage, our own faith, is a gift. Jesus asks us to share that gift. In sharing there is no diminishing of our own gift. On the contrary, our own gift is enhanced. That is so characteristic of God's ways. (Listen to Jesus.)

Colloquy: Thank you, Father, for the gift of my faith. Increase my faith so that it may always be a deep, operative faith of commitment. Teach me to be singleminded as you were.

SEVENTH REFLECTION

vv. 39-42 "Many Samaritans from that town believed in him on the strength of the woman's word of testimony. . . ."

Jesus called the Samaritan woman to a special apostolate. The wisdom of God is manifest. It was she who could bring the good news of salvation to her own people. The Samaritans would not accept a Jew, nor could their own leaders be disciples for they would have been considered heretics for accepting the teachings of a Jew. God's ways are not our ways. God chooses the little people, the most unlikely people in the eyes of the world to do his work (*I Cor. 1:27ff*). Jesus called the Samaritan woman to be a disciple. He conditioned her by leading her to a conversion and by revealing his divine wisdom to her. She was entering the third stage of discipleship—: commitment. She was so convinced of the truth of the message of Jesus that she hurried off to her own people. (Let Jesus fill you with his love.)

Colloquy: Lord Jesus, fill me with that dynamic commitment of faith so that I may radiate the love, peace and joy which only you can give. Help me to respond to love and become an apostle of love as the Samaritan woman did.

Some suggested passages for prayer which deal with Jesus' treatment of women.

John 8:1-11	"Nor do I condemn you. . . ."
Luke 10:38-42	Martha of Bethany
John 11:1-44	Mary of Bethany
Luke 7:36-50	Sinful Woman—"Your faith has been your salvation."
Luke 1:39-45	Elizabeth at the Visitation
Mark 5:25-34	Woman with a Hemorrhage

14 Up a Tree with Zacchaeus the Tax Collector

Jesus Knew His Heart
Luke 19:1-10

Jesus invites you to come with him as he enters Jericho. He asks you to look beyond the external appearances of the crowd pressing upon him. He asks you to try to search their hearts. Some came out of curiosity hoping to see signs and wonders; other came to hear his teaching; still others were drawn by his magnetic personality. Reflect on the heart of Jesus too in this episode. What is he saying about himself by his attitude toward sinners, by his loving concern for all who flock to him? As we listen with our whole being, we come to know Jesus as he really is.

FIRST REFLECTION

v. 2 "There was a man there named Zacchaeus, the chief tax collector and a wealthy man."

The name Zacchaeus is significant. It means the innocent one, or the pure one. This is quite surprising since tax collectors, as employees of the Roman government, were considered traitors to their own people. They were despised; hence they were often unjust and tried to accumulate a fortune in a short time since their tenure of office was frequently short-lived. Jesus saw beyond the externals and saw the heart of Zacchaeus. As God reminds us: "I, the Lord, alone probe the mind and test the heart, to reward everyone according to his ways . . . ." (*Jer. 17:10*). Zacchaeus was a lonely man. He longed for acceptance and love. Whether Zacchaeus was honest at all times, or whether his encounter with Jesus effected a sudden conversion in him, we do not know. All we know is that this meeting with Jesus certainly justified his name—the innocent one. (Be with Jesus as he meets Zacchaeus.)

Colloquy: Jesus, like Zacchaeus I am daily collecting my little taxes, be they a need for praise and popularity, a need to be heard or a need to have my own way. Lord, you know my heart. May my daily encounter with you in your Word change my "heart of stone" into a 'natural heart' as you promised through your prophet.

SECOND REFLECTION

vv. 3-4 "He was trying to see what Jesus was like . . . climbed a sycamore tree which was along Jesus' route, in order to see him."

Zacchaeus had a great longing to draw close to Jesus. The crowd would not yield to his entreaties because they hated him as a tax collector. They must have laughed at their success in preventing him from coming close to Jesus, or from even seeing him. However, Zacchaeus had such a great desire to see Jesus that he was not thwarted in his efforts. He climbed a sycamore tree. Even though climbing a sycamore was perhaps a little easier, because this tree sends out huge branches close to its base, the crowd ridiculed and jeered him as he struggled to climb high enough to see Jesus.

Zacchaeus was prepared to accept these insults, so great was his desire just to get a glimpse of Jesus. What faith! What perseverance he manifested! How much he wanted to get to know this Jesus who was a friend of tax collectors, prostitutes and sinners. (Rest in Jesus' presence.)

Colloquy: Jesus, how easily I am discouraged in my efforts to see and find you in all the people and events of my life. I give up so quickly. Zacchaeus, please pray for me that my desire to see Jesus may be as great as yours and that I, like you, might overcome any obstacles which would hinder me from seeing Jesus in all things.

THIRD REFLECTION

v. 5 "Zacchaeus, hurry down. I mean to stay at your house today."

Jesus must have heard the cynical laughter of the crowd. He heard their taunts as Zacchaeus was perched in the sycamore tree. Jesus will not permit anyone who is striving to come to him fail in their efforts if they are sincere. How lovingly and emphatically he turned to the tax collector. What love must have prompted this privileged request of Jesus: "I mean to stay at your house today." What consternation filled the crowd as they listened to Jesus' tender words to Zacchaeus! What envy must have surged up in their hearts! Jesus called him by name, "Zacchaeus."

What a thrill for Zacchaeus to be known personally by Jesus! He calls us by name: "Fear not, for I have redeemed you; I have called you by name: you are mine" (*Isaiah 43:1*). As we pray with his Word, let us hear him call us by name. (Listen to Jesus call you by name.)

Colloquy: Jesus, you want to come and stay with me but you are so sensitive. You do not force an entrance into my life. You wait for my invitation. Help me to set my priorities in order so that I will invite you first before all else.

FOURTH REFLECTION

v. 6 "He quickly descended, and welcomed him with delight."

The awareness of the presence of Jesus should always bring us delight. Zacchaeus received him with great joy. Imagine too how delighted Jesus must have been when Zacchaeus accepted his invitation. On another occasion a rich man approached Jesus and asked if he might follow him: "Jesus looked at him with love and told him . . . 'Go sell what you have . . . after that, come and follow me.' He went away sad . . . ." (*Mk. 10:17ff*). Jesus too must have been disappointed. However, Zacchaeus responded to the invitation of Jesus with great joy. How pleased Jesus must have been at this generous response. This gives us pause to reflect on how readily we respond to Jesus when he asks us to follow him, to love him, to accept his plans and designs for our lives. Jesus assures us that if we accept his invitation his Father will love us and they will come and make their dwelling place with us. (*Jn. 14:23*.) (Give Jesus yourself.)

Colloquy: Jesus, grant me the generosity to respond with delight to the promptings of your grace. Like you, help me to always say yes to the Father. Give me the joy and happiness found in giving rather than in receiving.

FIFTH REFLECTION

v. 7 "He has gone to a sinner's house as a guest."

Jesus wanted to be known as a friend of sinners. Sinners received him, accepted him, believed in him, loved him. In turn, Jesus brought them hope and encouragement. He gave them assurance of mercy, compassion, healing and forgiveness. All that was important to Jesus was the sacrament of the moment. He did not probe the past, nor did he demand guarantees for the future. He looked at the heart at that very moment and reached out in loving forgiveness to them. How graciously this is exemplified on Calvary as he assured the Good Thief: "I assure you: this day you will be with me in paradise" (*Luke 23:43*). We cannot fathom that kind of loving forgiveness. It is too much for us. What consolation and joy it brings to our hearts! How often Jesus must turn to the Father in our behalf: "Father, forgive them; they do not know what they are doing" (*Lk.* 23:34). (Experience his forgiveness flooding your whole being.)

Colloquy: Jesus, thank you for loving me so much that you were willing to lay down your life for me. Even more, you rose from the dead to share your divine life with me even during my earthly exile. Jesus, I love you too.

SIXTH REFLECTION

v. 8 "I give half my belongings, Lord, to the poor. If I have defrauded anyone in the least, I pay him back fourfold."

Even though Zacchaeus was a rich man, he certainly practiced the spirit of detachment. He went far beyond what the law required for restitution and also for gifts to the poor. This gives us a better insight into the heart of Zacchaeus. This attitude, this disposition, made him more receptive to Jesus and to what he was teaching. Zacchaeus was already reaching out in love to others, yet he was judged by his peers to be a sinner. Jesus was criticized for going to the house of a sinner. There are two great lessons in this verse. How readily we sit in judgment of others without really knowing their hearts. Secondly, Zacchaeus teaches us a genuine spirit of detachment in using his wealth to help others. (Let Jesus love you.)

Colloquy: Jesus, thank you for your Evangelist's report of this incident. What powerful lessons are contained therein for my edification and emulation. Grant me Zacchaeus' disposition of heart and the courage to follow in his footsteps.

SEVENTH REFLECTION

vv. 9-10 "Today salvation has come to this house. . . .

The Son of Man has come to search out and
save what is lost."

Zacchaeus was really an apostle. Not only he was
saved, but his whole household which must have been
rather numerous since he was a wealthy man with
many servants. Jesus also reminds us of his mission in
life. He has come to save sinners. We are aware of this
truth, yet it remains for many of us an intellectual truth.
Does it really penetrate our hearts? Do we hear Jesus
saying to us personally and individually that he loved
us so much that he came to save us? He would have
done so if we were the only person alive. He is speaking to us personally when he assures us: "There is no
greater love than this: to lay down one's life for one's
friends" (Jn. 15:13). Therefore, he instituted the Sacrament of Reconciliation in order to come to us, to forgive, heal and redeem us personally and individually.
His forgiveness might otherwise seem rather general
and universal. (Let his forgiving, healing love flood
your soul.)

Colloquy: Jesus, what can I say in the face of such
love! Thank you for forgiving and healing me over and
over again. Help me to realize that this is your glory to
redeem and to save. What mystery your love unfolds!

Some additional passages of Jesus dealing with sinners and tax collectors:

Matthew 9:9-13	"I have come to call, not the self-righteous, but sinners."
Luke 7:36-50	"Your sins are forgiven. . . ."
Luke 15:11-32	Prodigal Son—"Father, I have sinned against God and against you . . . ."
Mark 2:1-12	Paralytic—"My son, your sins are forgiven . . ."

15 Blind Bartimaeus

I Want To See
Mark 10:46-52

As we pray with God's Word we receive many fruits of which we are sometimes not even aware. As we pray, we often read between the lines to discover what Jesus was really like. There are frequent nuances and overtones which give us many insights into the kind of person Jesus is. As we relive this experience with Bartimaeus we discover how approachable, how loving, how concerned Jesus was not only about Bartimaeus, but also about us. Bartimaeus teaches us about our attitudes toward Jesus. This knowledge reaches deeper into the mystery of his infinite love for each one of us. Be with Jesus and let him be for you.

FIRST REFLECTION

v. 47 "On hearing that it was Jesus of Nazareth, he began to call out, 'Jesus, Son of David, have pity on me!' "

Bartimaeus recognized his own helplessness. He could do nothing about his blindness, yet he wanted so badly to see. This realization of his helplessness brought him to Jesus to implore him to use his divine power. We too are helpless, yet how frequently we flounder with our own inability. We are so slow to accept our inadequacy. Someone has said facetiously: "When all else fails, turn to God!" How often we find ourselves with that same attitude! When we recognize our poverty of spirit, then we are empty and receptive to what Jesus wants to give us. Our prayer highlights our dependence upon him. Jesus wants us to ask not only to recognize our own inability, but also to help us make our request more specific in our own minds. (Listen with your whole being.)

Colloquy: Lord Jesus, with Bartimaeus I plead: "Jesus, Son of David have pity on me." Jesus, I recognize my complete dependence upon you. I trust you, I know you will grant whatever I am prepared to receive.

SECOND REFLECTION

v. 48 "Many people were scolding him to make him keep quiet, but he shouted out all the louder, 'Son of David, have pity on me!' "

The crowd would have prevented Bartimaeus from getting to Jesus. We wonder why. Were they concerned about Jesus, or did they want to monopolize him? Did they look upon a blind beggar as an outcast not deserving of attention? When we try to approach Jesus in prayer, there are so many obstacles. There is a busyness about life which seems to block our way to Jesus. Our daily duties seem to make so many demands on our time and attention. There are some people who would prevent us from getting to Jesus either because they envy our relationship with him, or because they do not have the faith to believe in his abiding presence. Like the "many people" around Bartimaeus, there are those who would prevent our coming to Jesus. Like Bartimaeus, we must persevere in striving to come to him, and we must continue to shout "all the louder." (Be still and let Jesus come to you.)

Colloquy: Lord, keep my focus above the many obstacles which would prevent my coming to you. Do not permit the influence of others or preoccupation with the mundane to divert me from coming to you.

THIRD REFLECTION

v. 49 "Then Jesus stopped and said, 'Call him over.' "

Jesus loves us with an infinite love. He came into the world to manifest this love in the concrete; hence he always reached out to those in need. He always heard their cry above the noise of the crowd. His heart reached out to the pleas of Bartimaeus. Jesus had invited all to come to him when he said: "Come to me, all you who are weary and find life burdensome, and I will refresh you" (*Mt. 11:28*). How could he not hear the plaintive cry of Bartimaeus? How could he not hear our cry when we come to him with faith and trust? Like Bartimaeus we must go to him. Jesus is very sensitive to our free will. He will not impose himself upon us, yet how graciously and generously he responds when we do turn to him. Love longs to be translated into action. How Jesus longs to reach out in love to us! Jesus said to the people "Call him over." He also asks us to bring others to him that they might experience his love for them. (Take all your cares to Jesus.)

Colloquy: Jesus, you are inviting me all day long to "Come, follow you," to come to you in trials and difficulties. Keep me attuned to your call. Let me listen. Let me hear your voice above the din of the crowd. Keep me open and receptive to your will.

FOURTH REFLECTION

v. 49 "You have nothing to fear from him! Get up! He is calling you!"

How frequently we are encouraged in Sacred Scripture not to be afraid! How often Jesus himself tells us: "Don't be afraid!" or "Fear is useless" and in many other ways he advises us not to be fearful. Jesus wants us to trust him. He will never ask anything from us which is too difficult or too painful. Jesus loves us so much he does not want us to hesitate to come to him even though we seem to have failed him so often. We manifest our love for him by trusting him. St. John too advises us: "Love has no room for fear; rather, perfect love casts out all fear" (*I John 4:18*). Jesus himself says: "Do not let your hearts be troubled. Have faith in God and faith in me" (*John 14:1*). What joy, what reassurance, trust brings to us! (Place yourself in his hands.)

Colloquy: Jesus, how fearful I am at times because I do not fully trust you. Fill my heart with your divine love that I may step out in faith and trust.

FIFTH REFLECTION

v. 50 "He threw aside his cloak, jumped up and came to Jesus."

The response of Bartimaeus is most gratifying. He threw aside his cloak. A cloak was an indispensable garment for the Semite. It was his protection against cold. It was his bed at night, yet Bartimaeus discarded his cloak without hesitation. He teaches us how detached we must be if we wish to approach Jesus. Furthermore, he jumped up. There was no hesitation on his part. He did not know what Jesus was going to ask of him; nevertheless, he responded wholeheartedly to the invitation. He came to Jesus. How Jesus must have rejoiced at this response. How pleased Jesus was that he could respond to Bartimaeus' need. How eagerly he wanted to relieve Bartimaeus of his blindness after he accepted his invitation to come to him. (Be receptive to what Jesus asks.)

Colloquy: Lord Jesus, you invite me to come to you so that you can rid me of my blindness and my lack of faith but how I hesitate, wondering what you are going to ask of me. Grant me the gift of trust in you that I may respond graciously and generously to your inspirations and grace.

SIXTH REFLECTION

v. 50 "What do you want me to do for you?—'Rabboni, I want to see.' "

How much is implied in the request of Bartimaeus. Yes, he wanted his sight restored so that he could enjoy the beauty of life around him. He wanted to be like the rest of men. He did not enjoy begging and all the rejection that went with it. He wanted even more. Bartimaeus wanted the eyes of his faith opened so that he could really accept Jesus for what he was professed to be, the great Prophet and Messiah. How often we take our gift of sight for granted! How often do we really thank our loving Father for this gift? How frequently we take for granted the gift of our faith. (Open your whole being to receive his gifts.)

Colloquy: Jesus, what a touching prayer: "I want to see." Teach me to pray often for the gift of sight and insight so that I may have a deep, operative faith, that I may see your presence and power in all the events of my life. Thank you for the gift of my physical sight.

SEVENTH REFLECTION

v. 52 "Your faith has healed you."

Over and over again, Jesus asked for faith. He wants us to believe in him, to trust him, to commit ourselves to the way of life that he came to announce. When Jesus found faith, he was always pleased. How frequently he said that he was using his divine power because people believed in him. How plainly he said to Bartimaeus: "Your faith has healed you." Jesus wants us to accept him to such an extent that we are willing to commit ourselves to him. He wants us to live with a faith of expectancy which trusts God implicitly as our loving, gracious Abba. Faith is a gift of the Holy Spirit, but he will not force it upon us. Like any other gift, our faith will be strengthened and increased only as we use it. The more frequently we step out in faith, the stronger it becomes. (Renew your faith in Jesus.)

Colloquy: Jesus, when the disciples asked you why they could not cast out a devil, you answered "because you have so little trust." I pray with the father of the boy: "I do believe! Help my lack of trust!"

If you wish to continue praying about the healing power of Jesus, the following texts may be helpful:

Mark 8:22-26	"Can you see anything?"
John 9:1-39	"Since it was your eyes he opened, what do you have to say about him? 'He is a prophet.' "
Luke 7:18-28	"The blind recover their sight. . . ."
Matthew 9:27-31	"Because of your faith it shall be done to you."

16 A Paralytic

Jesus Is Touched By The Faith Of The Community
Mark 2:1-12

Jesus came into the world to prove to us, in reality
and in the concrete, how much the Father loves us and
how he himself loves us. At the very outset of his
public ministry, Jesus proved that love by reaching out
to heal every kind of suffering and pain. He healed
physically, psychologically and spiritually. He always
healed the whole person. There is not a single case on
record where Jesus ever refused to heal. Some, however, refused his healing. Jesus Christ is the same yesterday, today and forever (*Hebrews 13:8*). Jesus continues his healing ministry in our midst today. He
wants us, like the four men in the Gospel, to step out in
faith and trust and ask for his healing. Jesus was so
pleased with the faith of the community; he is equally
delighted with our faith.

FIRST REFLECTION

v. 3 "While he was delivering God's word to
them. . . ."

Jesus was singleminded. He had come to do the will
of the Father and that will was to bring the good news
to mankind. Jesus taught in season and out. He utilized
every opportunity to explain the good news.

Let us reflect momentarily on the good news. God
the Creator and Sustainer of the entire universe is

communicating with us. He is speaking to each one of us personally. In the Gospel Jesus tells us that his Father is a loving, provident, compassionate Abba. Jesus also tells us much about himself by his words, his actions and attitudes. ("Be still and know that I am your God.")

Colloquy: Father, I thank you for your Word, your revelation, your personal message to me. May it find a home in my heart.

SECOND REFLECTION

v. 3 "The four who carried him were unable to bring him to Jesus. . . ."

The men who performed this service to their fellow man were men of great faith. They believed that Jesus could heal. They manifested their loving concern for the paralytic by carrying him to Jesus. How far we do not know. It might have been a short distance; it could have been miles. Their loving concern was so great that they were not about to give up easily. They even opened up the roof in order to bring the sick man to Jesus. Perseverance was also a virtue of these kind men. ("Wait in patience and know that I am your God.")

Colloquy: Jesus, fill me with a loving concern for my brothers and sisters realizing that what we do to others you accept as being done to you.

THIRD REFLECTION

v. 5 "When Jesus saw their faith . . . ."

Jesus was moved to heal the paralyzed man because he was touched by the faith of the men who brought the cripple to him. We know nothing about the faith of the paralytic, but we do know that Jesus was overjoyed at the faith of the stretcher bearers. Jesus was always deeply moved by faith, and here it is the faith of the community which touched him. How precious to Jesus is our loving concern for the sick and suffering. How

Jesus loves them. Notice too how often the suffering radiates the joy of the Lord. Suffering usually brings us closer to Jesus and his loving Father. (Let Jesus speak to you through the suffering of others.)

Colloquy: Jesus increase my faith so that I may see you in all my less fortunate brothers and sisters. Thank you for granting me life and health of mind and body.

FOURTH REFLECTION

v. 5 "My son, your sins are forgiven."

At times Jesus was asked for a physical healing, but he often recognized the need for even greater healing. He healed the whole person. He wanted the paralytic not only to be physically well, but to have that interior peace and joy which comes from knowing that all is well between us and God.

Sin is the only barrier which robs us of the peace which a deep personal relationship with God brings. (Bask in God's forgiving love.)

Colloquy: Lord, let me hear with my whole being your consoling words: "My son, your sins are forgiven." Thank you for forgiving and healing me so many, many times.

FIFTH REFLECTION

v. 7 "He commits blasphemy!"

While Jesus was deeply moved by the dynamic faith of the men who brought the crippled man to him, how chilled he must have been by the lack of faith of some of the scribes who questioned his right to forgive sins. This is just another one of the many rejections which Jesus suffered throughout his earthly sojourn. Love must find expression in action. Jesus loved so much he was compelled to heal and forgive. How disappointed he must have been to be accused of blasphemy! How he wanted to win those hearts, yet they continued in their obstinacy! (Be close to Jesus as he heals you.)

Colloquy: Jesus, remove any barriers of doubt or hesitation as well as any obstacles which prevent me from seeing your love in all your actions.

SIXTH REFLECTION

v. 11 "I command you: Stand up! Pick up your mat and go home."

How firm and how accommodating Jesus was to this hostile group of scribes! He manifests his omnipotent power in such a dramatic way. He takes full control over the power of sin and evil, yet their minds and hearts were closed. Jesus came to break the power of evil. He came to expiate the sins of mankind. He came to forgive. Nothing was going to impede that mission given him by his Father. He proved beyond any shadow of a doubt that he could forgive sins and that he is God. There is no evidence in the Gospel that his actions convinced the scribes. How frustrating it must have been for Jesus. (Let his healing power surge through your whole being.)

Colloquy: Jesus, grant me the faith to be responsive to your presence and power in my life. Thank you too for forgiving me countless times when I said no to your love. I love you as my compassionate, merciful God.

SEVENTH REFLECTION

v. 12 "All gave praise to God . . . ."

The men of faith who carried the paralyzed man and the crowd who believed in Jesus gave praise and thanks to God for this powerful demonstration of his loving concern and compassionate forgiveness. What joy, what reassurance, this healing must have brought them. How their hearts rejoiced at the goodness of Jesus! Our solemn duty and our greatest privilege is to praise and thank God. Each day he works his wonders of loving concern in our lives. Each day we need to pause to be grateful and to use his gifts to the best of our ability. (Let your heart quietly sing his praises.)

Colloquy: Jesus, I praise you. I thank you. I adore you. I worship you. Above all, I love you and I want to love daily more and more. Thank you for loving me just as I am.

To continue praying with this theme of Jesus the Healer we suggest the following passages:

Luke 5:12-16	"Lord, if you will to do so, you can cure me."
Matthew 8:5-13	"I am not worthy to have you under my roof."
Mark 9:14-29	"I do believe! Help my lack of trust!"
Mark 7:31-37	"Ephphatha!—Be opened!"

17   Good Shepherd

Mine Know Me
John 10:1-18

If you had an opportunity to sit quietly in the shepherd's field near Bethlehem, or go rest on a Galilean hillside to watch a shepherd tend his sheep, then this verbal portrait of the Good Shepherd would speak eloquently to your heart. One must observe the loving concern of a shepherd for his sheep. His watchful eye never rests, but scans the environs at all times for any lurking danger to his sheep as well as to observe whether or not a sheep may be straying from the flock. The sheep love their shepherd and often go over to him to nudge him and receive an affectionate pat in return. When one observes the loving solicitude of the shepherd and the reciprocal attention of the sheep, then he can approach the Good Shepherd with faith and trust.

FIRST REFLECTION

vv. 1-3 "The sheep hear his voice as he calls his own by
        name . . . ."

In myriad ways Jesus tries to tell us who and what he is for us. He is our Good Shepherd. He is personally concerned about each one of us. In fact he speaks to us so often that he wants us to recognize his voice. Jesus does not say that we will hear his words, but rather his voice. There is something very personal about a voice.

Each voice has its own distinct tonality and timber. Secondly, Jesus calls us by name. It is flattering to hear someone call us by name. It means that person cares. The Good Shepherd cares so much that he leads us out to green pastures supplying all our needs. As we pray with these words, a comforting picture of Jesus reveals itself. (Listen to Jesus call you by name.)

Colloquy: Jesus, you often speak to me, but my hearing is not always attuned to your message because of my involvement in so many temporalities. Teach me to give you full attention each day in prayer and throughout the day.

SECOND REFLECTION

vv. 4-5 "He walks in front of them, and the sheep follow him because they recognize his voice."

When we are genuinely convinced that Jesus loves us with an infinite love, then we can easily place our full trust in him. Love trusts implicitly. Furthermore, love recognizes the voice of the person loved. According to the customs in the time of Jesus, the sheep were kept in a common corral at night. In the morning the shepherd would stand at the gate and call his own sheep by name. His sheep would recognize his voice and respond immediately. Even though he may call us to a heavy task, or to some obscure apostolate, we will trust him. Yes, we will recognize his voice. (Be with Jesus.)

Colloquy: Lord Jesus, teach me to trust you. You love me and could not permit anything to happen to me which is not for your greater honor and glory and my own welfare. Inculcate that lesson deep in my heart.

THIRD REFLECTION

vv. 7-10 "I came that they might have life and have it to the full."

In this moving statement Jesus gives us the summary of the whole mystery of Redemption. Jesus came not only to atone for our sins, but to raise us to a new life of sharing in his divine life. We are the temples of the Holy Spirit. Through the power of his Spirit, Jesus is dwelling within us. This is why he prayed to the Father "that they may be one, as we are one—I living in them, you living in me" (*John 17:22*). This is our real dignity in life: that Jesus is living in us and making us Christians in the true sense of the word. This gift of divine life is only the prelude to the fullness of that divine life which will be ours after death. Jesus' death gives meaning to our death. As Paul tells us: "Just as Christ was raised from the dead by the glory of the Father, we too might live a new life" (*Romans 6:4*). (Relax and experience his presence within you.)

Colloquy: Jesus, what greater gift could you have given me than the gift of yourself? Give me a deeper understanding of the mystery of your indwelling that I may respond in greater gratitude to you.

FOURTH REFLECTION

vv. 11-13 "I am the good shepherd; the good shepherd
lays down his life for the sheep."

Jesus not only told us that the good shepherd would lay down his life for his sheep, he actually did so. Did he not tell us: "There is no greater love than this: to lay down one's life for one's friends" (*Jn. 15:13*). The day after Jesus made this statement, he accepted the shame and the pain of death by crucifixion. Jesus also reminds us that unless the grain of wheat falls into the ground and dies, it remains alone; but in death to self, it produces a rich harvest. Again Jesus tells us that if we wish to be his disciples we need to take up our cross daily and follow him, our good shepherd. Do we hear the voice of Jesus in the crosses and trials which come our way? Even though the spirit is willing and the flesh cries out in rebellion, we are still the sheep recognizing the voice of our shepherd. (Relive with Jesus the total gift of himself for our salvation.)

Colloquy: Lord Jesus, too often I think about the price of discipleship and what it entails in following you as a docile sheep. Remind me of the precious fruits which come from following you. Keep my focus on you for your yoke is easy and your burden light.

FIFTH REFLECTION

vv. 14-15 "I know my sheep and my sheep know me. . . ."

The hired hand was invited into discipleship and even into the role of shepherd, but he was hesitant about making a full commitment. He saw the price as too much, the risk as too great. We are reminded of the rich man who loved Jesus and wanted to follow him, but was unwilling "to go sell what he had." The Father too complains about the shepherds who tend the sheep for their own selfish ends and desert the sheep in times of danger (*Ezekiel 34*). The Father said that he himself would care for his sheep, pasture them, give them rest, seek them out, bind up the injured, etc. The Father does that for us, his sheep, through Jesus the Good Shepherd. How eager Jesus is to fulfill that role of shepherd! (Reflect on the Father's care of you.)

Colloquy: Thank you, Jesus, for shepherding me through thick and thin, for leading me to the green pastures of your love, for shielding me from my worst enemy: myself. Help me to "know" you better and be attuned to your loving solicitude.

SIXTH REFLECTION

v. 16 "I have other sheep that do not belong to this fold."

How the heart of Jesus must ache for those who are not of his fold! They do not belong either because they do not know him or because they have never felt his presence nor experienced his love. These sheep might not have had the privileges which are ours. Our mission in life is to bring the good news to them, not so much as revealed truth, but by the witness of our own lives. As we permit the love, peace and joy of Jesus to radiate through us, they will begin to know him. Secondly, these sheep do not belong because they might have lost their way and strayed far from the flock. Jesus tells us of his loving concern for the lost sheep. He was willing to risk losing ninety-nine in the desert in order to search for the one that was lost. Notice too how lovingly and gently he carries it home on his shoulders. Then he tells us that there will be more joy in heaven over one repentant sinner than over ninety-nine who have no need to repent (*Luke 15:3-7*). (Thank Jesus for selecting you to be one of his sheep.)

Colloquy: Jesus, what hope and courage you hold out to me knowing, as I now do, that you deal so lovingly and gently with sinners. Help me to turn to you with genuine repentance and to be open to receive your healing, forgiving love at all times.

SEVENTH REFLECTION

vv. 17-18 "The Father loves me for this: that I lay down my life to take it up again."

Jesus freely laid down his life because he loves us so deeply. Jesus had experienced the perfect love of the Father in the mystery of the Trinity. Furthermore, he loves us with an infinite love. Prompted and motivated by this love he could do nothing less than give the total gift of himself, down to the very last drop of blood. In all of this he is not a helpless victim of his enemies. No, this is the free gift of himself. With his divine power he could have struck dead all those who threatened his life. Love prevailed. He did have the power to take it up again, and even to impart that divine life to us. What greater love, what more tender care than that of the Good Shepherd for us his sheep! (Let Jesus fill your heart with his love.)

Colloquy: Thank you for being my shepherd. Help me to penetrate the mystery of your love. Keep me receptive so that I may become the channel of your love to other sheep, especially those who do not know you.

Other scriptural passages which help us pray with this same theme:

Luke 15:1-7	"Rejoice with me because I have found my lost sheep."
Ezekiel 34:11-24	"I myself will look after and tend my sheep."
John 21:15-19	"Feed my lambs . . . Feed my sheep."

18 The Vine and the Branches

My Friend Had A Vineyard
John 15:1-8

In a brief but picturesque allegory Jesus explains the tremendous mystery of his indwelling in each of us. At the moment of our Baptism we became the temples of the Holy Spirit. Jesus is living in us through the power of the Holy Spirit. Love seeks union and Jesus explains his indwelling in this simple, but profound figure of speech. He loves us so much that he is living within us. (Rest with Jesus in the midst of the vineyard and listen to his words. Let the mystery of this profound truth sink into the very depth of your being.)

FIRST REFLECTION

v. 1 "I am the true vine and my Father is the vine-grower."

Jesus is the source of our divine life. He is dwelling within us, loving us, strengthening us, filling us with himself. He is the true vine; we are the branches. It is impossible for a branch to live without being attached to the vine. Jesus dwelling within us makes us children of the Father. It is this which gives us our dignity as Christians. Since Jesus is the wellspring of our divine life, we are all united in one family, one community with him. (Sit with Jesus on a Galilean hillside amid vines bearing luscious grapes.)

Colloquy: Jesus, how can I ever fathom this mystery

of your love? Help me to comprehend my own dignity as well as the dignity of my brothers and sisters.

SECOND REFLECTION

v. 2 "He prunes away every barren branch, but the fruitful ones he trims clean to increase their yield."

A pruning process can be painful. However it is necessary to improve the fruit. Shoots, called suckers, grow on various trees and shrubs. They drain strength from the plant and they do not bear any fruit. Pruning is essential if the tree is to bear good fruit. Our loving Father, likewise, knows what is best for us, what will help us yield fruit in abundance. Does he not say to us: "I know well the plans I have in mind for you . . . plans for your welfare not for woe!" Like Jesus who was not alternately yes and no but was always yes to the Father, so we must live our yes in trust to our loving Abba even though the pruning may cause pain. (Let Jesus point out the areas which need pruning.)

Colloquy: Jesus, grant me the wisdom and courage to say yes always to you, realizing that many neon gods can readily replace you. May my life center around you as my primary priority at all times.

THIRD REFLECTION

v. 3 "You are clean already, thanks to the word I have spoken to you."

There is great power in God's Word. It has a cleansing power even though we may not always be aware of its purifying action. Paul tells us "The word is near you, on your lips and in your heart" (*Romans 10:8*). As we pray with his Word, as we expose our thoughts and attitudes to his Word, we recognize our own rationalizations, we see how far our thinking may be from the thoughts and attitudes of Jesus. Our loving Father assures us that his Word will achieve the end for which he sent it (*Isaiah 55:10ff*). As we pray with his Word each day, the conversion process is continually taking place within us. (Rest quietly in his presence.)

Colloquy: Jesus, I need healing and purification in so many areas of life. As I pray with your Word, make me receptive to the purifying and the healing power of that Word. Grant me that special grace.

FOURTH REFLECTION

v. 4 "Live on in me, as I do in you."

What a comforting mystery! Jesus fills us with his love. He wants us to bask in his love. Just as the sun nourishes us, warms us, brightens our day, so his love envelops us and fills us. The fruit which Jesus wants the branch to bear is to permit his love to be channeled through us to others, to radiate the sunshine of his love to all he sends across our path. Only through his presence and power within us can we accomplish this mission in life. Jesus asks us to become channels that will permit him to reach out in love to others. This makes loving our neighbor a little easier. Jesus asks us to be simply an empty pipeline and to let him work through us. Then we can come along with him. (Bask in the warmth of his love.)

Colloquy: Jesus, how overwhelming the realization and awareness of you dwelling within me! Teach me to relate to your presence within me in everything I do. Yes, "let me live on in you."

FIFTH REFLECTION

v. 5 "I am the vine, you are the branches."

Jesus is the vine, the very source of life, of power, of love, of fruitfulness. Furthermore, just as the branch blossoms out and eventually bears the fruit so does Jesus permit us to "produce abundantly" provided we live in him. Unfortunately, we are so pelagian in our thinking. We launch out on our own as though everything depended on us. Nevertheless, how gentle Jesus is when we fail. He simply reminds us again and again: "Apart from me you can do nothing" and continues to empower us. (Listen to the power of Jesus present in you.)

Colloquy: Jesus, continue to fill me with the awareness of your loving presence and power within me. Thank you for empowering me so often without my even being aware of it.

SIXTH REFLECTION

v. 6 "A man who does not live in me is like a withered, rejected branch, picked up to be thrown in the fire and burnt."

The dead branch of a vine is worthless. It cannot be used for lumber, a walking stick or for any other practical purpose; it can only be gotten rid of by burning. What an image of our own personal value and usefulness without the indwelling of Jesus! Our pride, our self-centeredness often block what God wants to do in us and through us. This is why we must stay attached to the vine so that the life of Jesus can flow in us and through us. (Rest quietly and let the divine life of Jesus surge through your whole being.)

Colloquy: Jesus, the choice is mine. I'm either a withered branch fit to be burned, or a fruit-bearing branch. Show me how to bear fruit and keep me faithful.

SEVENTH REFLECTION

v. 8 "My Father has been glorified in your bearing much fruit and becoming my disciples."

When we become a disciple of Jesus, we not only wish to follow in his footsteps, but we wish to be identified more closely with him. Our thoughts should be his thoughts, our attitudes his attitudes and our reactions should be in harmony with the mind of Christ. The glory of the Father is the work of salvation which is being carried on in us through the indwelling of Jesus and through the power of the Holy Spirit. As the Spirit sanctifies us and purifies us we are giving glory to God. (Bask in his love and let Jesus continue to fill you.)

Colloquy: Jesus, you prayed so fervently that I could be one with you. This identification can be effected only through your presence and power within me. Make me pliable clay in your loving hands.

If you wish to continue to pray about this tremendous mystery of Jesus' indwelling within us, we suggest the following passages:

John 17:20-26	"I pray that they may be one in us. . . ."
John 14:1-24	"We will come to him and make our dwelling place with him."
Isaiah 5:1-7	Vineyard Song—"What more was there to do for my vineyard—that I had not done?"
Psalm 80:1-20	"A vine from Egypt you transplanted. . . ."

19 Jesus Feeds The Multitude

The Lad Who Shared His Lunch
John 6:1-15

Rest with Jesus in warm spring sunshine on this Galilean hillside. As you sit with a brilliant carpet of millions of wild flowers surrounding you, observe what is taking place. Pilgrims are moving from the north toward Jerusalem. They have heard much about Jesus, the great Prophet come to save his people. Perhaps they have never seen him. Suddenly they find him here, lovingly reaching out to all who come to him. His teachings fill them with hope and joy. His magnetic personality holds them spellbound. The joy which floods their hearts cannot be described. They forget their hunger, their fatigue. Live these precious moments with Jesus.

FIRST REFLECTION

v. 2 "A vast crowd kept following him because they saw the signs he was performing for the sick."
The people who lived at the time of Jesus were very much like us. They were eager and hungry to hear the Word of God. They needed assurance that they were loved by God. They recognized in Jesus a great prophet who could reveal the love of the Father for them. They were sick, troubled, anxious. Jesus came to heal suffering and affliction. They wanted to be close to Jesus, to hear his Word, to experience his love reaching out to

them. There was something so special about him, they just could not leave him. They stayed and stayed in spite of their hunger and fatigue. (Sit close to Jesus on that Galilean hillside.)

Colloquy: Jesus, I want to follow you. I want to be close to you. I need to hear you tell me that you do love me and are concerned about me. Keep me ever aware of your abiding presence with me and within me which makes you closer to me than you were to these people on this day in Galilee.

SECOND REFLECTION

v. 5 "Where shall we buy bread for these people to eat?"

The loving concern of Jesus reflects itself in his desire to supply the physical needs of these people. They were loyal to him and had followed him for a long time. He knew they were hungry. He felt their physical hunger as well as their spiritual hunger for a deeper relationship with God. He asked Philip this question, simply to test his faith and his attitude toward these people. Jesus turns to us to ask our help in the apostolate. He tests us to show us our own mentality and attitude, not to embarrass us, but to indicate to us our strength or weakness so that, with his help, we may be transformed. (As you sit at Jesus' feet, answer his question to you.)

Colloquy: Jesus, Lord of heaven and earth, you come to me as you did to Philip—to test me. How often you find me wanting! Teach me your loving concern for others in which I will find true joy and happiness.

THIRD REFLECTION

v. 7 "Not even with two hundred days' wages could we buy loaves enough to give each of them a mouthful!"

In this response Philip manifested his own poverty

of spirit. He had to admit that it was virtually impossible for them ever to feed so large a group. That is precisely what Jesus wanted. When we recognize our own inadequacy, our own inability to accomplish anything by ourselves, then Jesus comes to our rescue. As long as we insist on doing everything ourselves, he lets us go until we experience our own helplessness, then he takes over. He also told us: "How blest are the poor in spirit." However, if we are blest with a little, like this young lad, then Jesus wants us to be generous so that he can multiply our little into much, very much. (Offer Jesus the little you have.)

Colloquy: Jesus, you told me in no uncertain terms that "apart from me, you can do nothing." Keep me humble so that this truth becomes the norm of my life—to strive as though everything depends on me, but to pray as though everything depends on you.

FOURTH REFLECTION

v. 10 "Get the people to recline."

The reaction of the people to this request was phenomenal. These people were tired, restless, hungry. They wanted to be on their way in search of food. This request to recline on the ground meant that they were asked to place all their trust and confidence in Jesus. It meant that they were submitting themselves totally to him. This required great faith. How pleased Jesus must have been to witness such faith in him. His heart must have leaped with joy. St. Mark adds his own little touch when he says: "The people took their places in hundreds and fifties, neatly arranged like flower beds (*Mark 6:40*). I am sure they must have looked that way to Jesus also. (Be docile and sit with Jesus.)

Colloquy: Lord, grant me that gift of faith that responds immediately to your voice regardless of how impractical or impossible your request may seem. May my response in faith cheer your heart always.

FIFTH REFLECTION

v. 11 "Jesus then took the loaves of bread, gave thanks, and passed them around to those reclining there; he did the same with the dried fish, as much as they wanted."

How often Jesus spends time in prayer, thanking his Father for his goodness, his loving providential care. Jesus prayed often as was his custom. He gave thanks to his Father for the gift of these loaves and also for the sign and wonder which was about to take place. We take so much for granted. God is so good to us. How plentifully he supplies all our needs. He gives us every breath as well as every morsel of food. When we are grateful to God for his gifts and use them well, we can be sure that his gifts will flow in superabundance, especially those which help us carry on our mission in life. (Sit at Jesus' feet and count your blessings from the time of your birth.)

Colloquy: Jesus, thank you for teaching me how important gratitude is. Keep me ever aware of your loving kindness and make my heart a grateful heart.

SIXTH REFLECTION

v. 12 "Gather up the crusts that are left over so that nothing will go to waste."

How careful Jesus is with the gifts of his Father. Nothing may go to waste. What a valuable lesson he teaches us, when he shows us how to handle the gifts of his Father, especially the graces he showers so generously upon us. Furthermore, Jesus knew that in our human weakness we would need proof of his divine power in multiplying the loaves. How considerate, how accommodating, how condescending to our doubting minds. This manifestation of his divine power was an ideal preparation for and a strengthening of our faith to accept the Holy Eucharist. (Sit in the presence of Jesus and try to comprehend what all this means.)

Colloquy: Jesus, how carefully and how meticulously you prepared us for the greatest of all gifts, the gift of yourself in the Holy Eucharist. You demonstrated your power over bread to prepare us for your tremendous love offering: the gift of yourself under the appearance of bread.

SEVENTH REFLECTION

vv. 14-15 "When the people saw the sign he had performed . . . Jesus realized that they would come and carry him off to make him king, so he fled back to the mountain alone."

Through the prophet Isaiah, God says to us: "My thoughts are not your thoughts, nor are your ways my ways." In this event the people saw a man of great power who could free them from the domination of Rome, who could restore the Kingdom of Israel to its pristine glory. Jesus came to offer them so much more—not just an earthly kingdom, but a kingdom which would bring peace and joy to their present lives, which would be a preparation for that eternal union with him and the Father. Earthly glory could never satisfy his divine heart, nor would an earthly kingdom meet the real needs of these his people. Jesus was anxious to be alone with his Father in solitude and prayer. Only in prayer can we establish the real values in our lives. Jesus shows us the way. (Go to the mountain with Jesus in silence.)

Colloquy: Jesus, your actions speak louder than words. Teach me how to come to prayer and there find the proper priorities in my life. Keep my gaze ever fixed on you. Lead me to the mountain many times in my workaday world.

Similar demonstrations of God's loving providential care are found in:

131

Exodus 16:1-15	"This is the bread which the Lord has given you to eat."
John 2:1-11	"People usually serve the choice wine first. . . ."
Matthew 14:13-21	"He took the five loaves and two fish, looked up to heaven, blessed and broke them. . . ."

20 The Transfiguration

The Tops Of The Mountains Are His
Luke 9:28-36

Mount Tabor is a perfectly shaped sugarloaf mountain. It is situated in the middle of a beautiful and fertile plain. In fact, it is surrounded on all sides by spacious plains reaching out in every direction. It rises majestically above the valley floor to form a natural altar. Jesus went up this mountain to pray. There he was strengthened to give his total yes to the Father. Mount Tabor lays claim to being the first Christian altar because on its summit Jesus made the total oblation of himself for the salvation of mankind. The top of that mountain became resplendent with the indescribable brilliance of his divine presence radiating through his humanity. That celestial radiance will also reflect in our hearts as we too are able to say our yes to the Father.

FIRST REFLECTION

v. 28 · "He took Peter, John and James, and went up onto a mountain to pray."

These three apostles seem to have been Jesus' favorites. We can think of many reasons for this. Possibly they accepted Jesus with greater faith and perhaps their love for him was more intense than that of the other disciples. Perhaps their faith and love made them more committed to him and his mission. These three were also his special prayer team. When Jesus went to raise the daughter of Jairus to life, "he permitted no one to enter with him except Peter, John, James, and the child's parents (*Luke 8:51*). Jesus wanted the prayer support of these apostles. Besides this solemn occasion on Mt. Tabor he was yet to invite them into the Garden where he endured the traumatic agony. Jesus wanted those nearest and dearest to him to be with him and to support him in these critical moments. Furthermore, the transfiguration was to prepare them to become stalwart pillars of faith when he and his mission would seem to go down in utter defeat. (Pray with Jesus on the mountain.)

Colloquy: Jesus, take me with you and be very present to me at all times, but especially during those critical moments when my faith might be tested. May I come to you often in prayer that you may give me all the reassurance which my weak human nature requires.

SECOND REFLECTION

v. 29 "While he was praying, his face was changed in appearance and his clothes became dazzlingly white."

Jesus teaches us a vitally important lesson. It was while he was praying that he was able to say his unreserved yes to the Father.

He gave himself willingly and unconditionally to endure all the dreadful pain, rejection and humiliation which was yet to come in his ministry. The Father was so pleased with this total *kenosis* on the part of Jesus that he permitted the glory of Jesus to radiate through his humanity. Prayer helps us to see more clearly the will of God. Prayer is a means of making us receptive to what God wishes to do in us and through us. Prayer helps us to give ourselves totally to what God may ask of us. While praying Jesus was better able to say yes to his Father. In prayer we too will be better able to say our yes to our loving Abba. (Rest quietly with Jesus in prayer.)

134

Colloquy: Lord Jesus, with your apostles I ask you: "Lord, teach us to pray." Help me to find the solitude of a mountain top in my own environment that I might open myself completely to what you want to say to me and how you want me to respond to your inspirations. Teach me to listen intently.

THIRD REFLECTION

v. 30 "Suddenly two men were talking with him— Moses and Elijah."

Our heavenly Father is so accommodating. He knows our human weaknesses—how frail our faith is, how hard it is for us to accept his plans. Here he permits Moses and Elijah to appear to show us the continuity of his salvific plan. Moses represents the Law which bound the Chosen People into a covenant which made them the people of God. Elijah shows us that all the prophets held out hope and promise for the salvation of mankind. Their presence at the transfiguration manifests to us that the Law and the Prophets are fulfilled in Jesus. Now Jesus must carry out the final act of redemption by his passion and death. This ephiphany prepares us for the final act in this divine drama. How gracious of our loving Father! (Rest close to the three apostles and witness this divine manifestation.)

Colloquy: Father, you are our gracious and loving Abba. You make yourself so immanent in Jesus so that our faith may be strengthened. Make my faith dynamic and operative in my life. Endow me with a genuine, expectant faith so that my whole life may be pleasing to you.

FOURTH REFLECTION

v. 31 "They appeared in glory and spoke of his passage, which he was about to fulfill in Jerusalem."

Already a growing wave of intrigue, jealousy, envy,

hatred and rejection was moving in upon Jesus. He was soon to be put to death because he would not change one iota of the Father's message—the good news of salvation. This was difficult to understand.

Jesus came to give us the greatest gift he could possibly give, the gift of eternal life. "I came that they might have life and have it to the full" *(John 10:10)*. In spite of this, the opposition was mounting against him. Moses and Elijah gave Jesus and us the assurance that all this was according to God's saving plan for us. We need to have that confirmation. With our finite minds and our myopic vision he would not be able to fit all the pieces of the jigsaw puzzle together. How good God is to help us understand! (Let the full impact of this event settle into your heart.)

Colloquy: Father, thank you for your solicitude in helping us to understand your mysterious ways. Please give me the reassurance of your tender and loving concern when suffering, pain and rejection come into my life. Continue to reveal your providential care.

FIFTH REFLECTION

v. 33 "Master, how good it is for us to be here."

Peter and his companions were overwhelmed by the powerful manifestation of the presence and divinity of Jesus. It was a profound contemplative experience. They could not grasp it fully. All Peter could say was "How good it is for us to be here," but how significant was that outpouring of his heart. Notice that the three apostles first spent time in prayer with Jesus which helped them to become receptive to all that was taking place. They did not panic, nor were they skeptical. They were simply overawed. As we spend time in prayer, we too rid ourselves of much of the sordid and mundane in our lives so that we can be open and receptive to what God is trying to accomplish in us. We recognize his signs more easily in quiet prayer. (Let your heart tell Jesus how good it is to be with him.)

Colloquy: Jesus, as I come to be with you, permit me to experience the power of your presence and the warmth of your love. Give me a longing and a hunger to be with you often in prayer. Fill my heart with that peace and joy which only you can give.

SIXTH REFLECTION

v. 35 "This is my Son, my Chosen One. Listen to him."

How gracious of the Father to confirm the mission of suffering, and ultimately death, which Jesus had to endure. There is so much mystery involved in suffering that our minds cannot grasp its purpose. Furthermore, the apparent defeat and death of Jesus would shock the world of his time. The Father understands our humanness which cannot possibly comprehend the meaning and necessity of the death of Jesus. Just as the Father had confirmed the teaching mission of Jesus at the time of his Baptism, now he confirms the mystery of his "passage." Repeatedly the Word of God pleads with us to "listen." Once again the Father begs us to listen to Jesus. Listening is a prayer posture. We must listen with our hearts when God speaks to us through suffering. (Listen with your whole being to what God is saying to you today.)

Colloquy: Lord Jesus, my mind is so cluttered most of the time. Teach me to listen as your Father instructed me to do. May my time of prayer be a quiet time of listening to you because I know you have so much to say to me.

SEVENTH REFLECTION

v. 36 "The disciples kept quiet, telling nothing of what they had seen at that time to anyone."

How impossible it is to speak about an experiential awareness of God's loving presence. When we experience God, we want to be still, alone, silent. At the very core of silence, we find God. Words are such lifeless vehicles of thought. They cannot possibly capture the experience. The disciples could not possibly convey to anyone what they had experienced. An attempt to try to share this experience would have been futile and frustrating. They needed to let the experience be integrated into their own lives so that when the crisis did come they could face it without trepidation. For those who have experienced God's love, no words are necessary; for those who have not experienced it, no words can convey it. (Let the experience of God sink deep into your heart in solitude.)

Colloquy: Jesus, I want to meet you in prayer. I want to experience your presence and feel your love. I know this is a special gift from you, but I need it from time to time to keep my focus always on you.

To continue to pray with this theme, you may find the following scriptural texts helpful:

II Peter 1:12-19	"For we were eyewitnesses of his sovereign majesty."
Mark 9:2-8	"He was transfigured before their eyes . . . ."
I Kings 19:1-18	"After the fire there was a tiny whispering sound."

21 Palm Sunday

Messianic Entry Into Jerusalem
Luke 19:28-44

Some time ago a movie attempting to portray the life
of Jesus presented the scene of his triumphant entry
into Jerusalem in a rather unique way. Jesus was all
alone riding on a white donkey. His way wended
through a section of a city in which the streets were
narrow and unpaved. The homes were dingy and re-
sembled a refugee camp. As Jesus was riding into the
city he was soliloquizing about the futility of his mission. Each time a note of discouragement would arise
on his lips, the white donkey would stop, turn and
raise his head to look at Jesus. After a little pat on his
neck the donkey would continue his journey. This
scene was rich in symbolism.

FIRST REFLECTION

v. 30 "Go into the village straight ahead of you."

This clear instruction shows the divine knowledge
which Jesus had. His exact directives, his foreknowledge of what to anticipate must have impressed those
who heard them. Obviously this was divine knowledge. The donkey was the mount which princes used
when they entered a city peacefully and joyfully. The
donkey is not a war mount. It was no threat to the
populace. Solomon rode a donkey to his coronation.
Jesus was saying that his messianic kingdom is one of

139

peace and joy. Jesus himself promised us: "Peace is my farewell to you, my peace is my gift to you" *(John 14:27)*. How Jesus longed to bring that peace to the Holy City! How Jesus desires to give us his peace! (Reflect on the thoughts which absorbed Jesus as he rode into Jerusalem.)

Colloquy: Jesus, thank you for the peace you share so generously with me. Let me continue to experience your peace more fully each day. Help me to proclaim in my own little way your kingdom of peace.

SECOND REFLECTION

v. 31 "Why are you untying the beast? . . . The Master has need of it."

The owner of the donkey was probably a disciple of Jesus since he immediately permitted his beast to be used by Jesus. As God, Jesus could have amply called upon his divine power to supply a donkey for this procession. However, he invites us to share in his ministry, and in his plans he depends upon us, his creatures, for help. He calls upon us, his disciples, to fulfill our task in the economy of salvation. How condescending! How privileged we are! Doesn't he permit the branch to bear fruit even though he is the vine? (What is Jesus asking of you today?)

Colloquy: Jesus, you call upon me to fulfill a special role in your divine plan. Grant me the eyes of faith to recognize your will and the courage and generosity to fulfill it to the letter even though I may not understand it at the moment. Thank you for inviting me.

THIRD REFLECTION

v. 36 "They spread their cloaks on the roadway as he moved along."

Like Solomon, Jesus did not permit them to crown him at this time. His kingdom was not of this world; an earthly coronation would have been meaningless. Secondly, his kingdom would not come until he had conquered sin and death. However, the people did accord him regal honors as they spread their cloaks before him and waved palm branches in this triumphant procession. Jesus did accept this proclamation on the part of the people as a preparation for his coming reign as king. Jesus' chief concern was always for the *anawim*. His entry into Jerusalem was likewise in the style of the simple, humble people. (In your contemplative prayer proclaim Jesus king of your heart.)

Colloquy: Lord Jesus, reign as king in my heart. Always walk with me that I may keep my eyes fixed on you and never be influenced by the secular standards around me. May my heart sing your praises with all my brothers and sisters throughout the world and with the celestial choir for all eternity.

FOURTH REFLECTION

v. 37 "The entire crowd of disciples began to rejoice and praise God loudly for the display of power they had seen . . . ."

The power of Jesus was so evidently divine that the people could not contain themselves. They had just witnessed Lazarus being raised to life. They had seen the many miracles of healing around them daily. Certainly Jesus did not manifest his power for human acclaim. He loved so much that he wanted to relieve all pain and suffering. He wanted people to believe in him. He hoped this "display of power" would achieve that purpose. Surely God was visiting his people. They naturally rejoiced by singing the Hallel Psalms in praising and thanking God. When we experience God's loving concern and power operative in our own lives, we cannot refrain from rejoicing and praising him, and responding to that great love. (Let your heart quietly and contemplatively sing his praises.)

Colloquy: Jesus, your presence and power is so

apparent in my daily living, if I only pause to reflect. May your power move me to a greater trust in you. May I daily praise you for your loving concern and power.

FIFTH REFLECTION

v. 38 "Blessed is he who comes as king in the name of the Lord!"

These words of the psalmist are personalized in Jesus. He is our king—a king who unites his subjects "with bands of love." At the birth of Jesus the angels announced, "a savior has been born to you, the Messiah and Lord." The theme of this angelic chorus is re-echoed here on Palm Sunday: "Peace in heaven and glory in the highest." Jesus came as prince of peace. His kingdom is one of peace and love and not one of might and power. How appropriate that we are reminded of this truth as Jesus enters the Holy City. Jesus wants to enter our hearts in the same triumphant way if we will but welcome him and open the door of our hearts to him. Did he not say: "Here I stand, knocking at the door."? (Be still and let his peace permeate your whole being.)

Colloquy: Jesus, I want you to be king of my heart and always the number-one priority in my life. Teach me to keep my vision ever riveted on you when the mundane demands around me seem so important and especially when they would wean me away from you.

SIXTH REFLECTION

v. 39 "Teacher, rebuke your disciples."

The Pharisees who asked Jesus to stop his disciples might have been friendly toward Jesus, but they might not have understood why he was accepting these regal and divine honors. They did not understand the honor being paid to Jesus for he had not yet accomplished the victory which they were expecting him to gain. It was only after his Resurrection that the happening of Palm

Sunday could be understood. Jesus won his victory over sin and death and truly he is king of the entire universe: heaven, hell and earth. Jesus' reply to the Pharisees was really a prophecy: "If they were to keep silence, I tell you the very stones would cry out." There were others in the crowd who hated Jesus and their objection was motivated by this hatred seething in their hearts. (Try to feel the opposition as Jesus might have felt it.)

Colloquy: How fortunate I am, Jesus, to see the whole paschal mystery in its entirety! I can better understand what was taking place on this occasion. How my heart sighs knowing the infinite love which compelled you to give all. Let me be truly grateful all the days of my life.

SEVENTH REFLECTION

v. 41 "Coming within sight of the city, he wept over it. . . ."

Suddenly the singing stopped. Jesus was weeping. How precious the Holy City with its Temple must have been to Jesus! How his heart ached knowing the destruction which was about to lay Jerusalem in ruins because they refused to believe in him. How scalding must those tears have been since he loved his own people so passionately. The word *Jerusalem* means "peaceful" yet how far from peace it was. With the psalmist Jesus pleads with us to pray for the new Jerusalem: "Pray for the peace of Jerusalem! . . . May peace be within your walls . . . . Peace be within you!" (*Psalm 122*). (Watch the tears of Jesus fall.)

Colloquy: Jesus, teach me to weep for my own indifference to your great love. You want to make your dwelling with me and within me as the very source of peace, yet I am so distracted, so unaware at times. Thank you always for your loving concern.

Additional texts which speak of the kingship of Jesus:

I Kings 1:28-37	"Mount my son Solomon upon my own mule and escort him down to Gihon."
John 6:14-15	"Jesus realized that they would come and carry him off to make him king. . . ."
John 18:33-38	"Are you the King of the Jews?"

22 The Last Supper

I Myself Am The Bread Of Life
Luke 22:7-20

As we walk into any church, be it a magnificent cathedral or a small, country parish church, we experience a sense of sacredness, an awareness of presence, an atmosphere of awe and reverence. This is not only a Christian faith experience, it is also felt by those who do not necessarily believe in the Real Presence. Surely "God has visited his people" and furthermore he has "made his dwelling among us." A person who loves wants to be near the person he loves. Jesus is no exception. He came not as a guest, but to stay. In the Eucharist he gives tangible evidence of his dwelling among us. His presence is appropriately called a Eucharistic Presence which means thanksgiving and that is precisely what this mystery elicits in us—a sense of gratitude. "Blessed be the Lord the God of Israel because he has visited and ransomed his people."

FIRST REFLECTION

v. 8 "Jesus sent Peter and John off with the instruction, 'Go and prepare our Passover supper for us'."
   As the earthly sojourn of Jesus was drawing to a close he wanted to give the apostles and us a memorial of his presence with us. He sent Peter and John to prepare the Passover meal. He wanted them to be a part of the great

gift he was about to give. He wanted to make them receptive to what he was about to do. Again Jesus manifested his divine foreknowledge. He told them exactly what they would find: the man carrying a water jar, the guest room and the hospitality they would receive. Once again Jesus wanted them to realize his divine knowledge to prepare them for the dreadful days ahead when their faith would be tested. Furthermore, he wanted them to play a role in this great banquet and to feel a part of it. (Listen to Jesus guide you by the inspirations of his grace.)

Colloquy: Jesus, how eager and anxious you were to give us the gift of yourself in the Eucharist. Help me to prepare myself well before I come to you in the Eucharist so that I may be disposed to appreciate your Eucharistic presence. Thank you for your gift.

SECOND REFLECTION

v. 14 "When the hour arrived, he took his place at the table, and the apostles with him."

In these few simple words the evangelist tells us of the most historic banquet ever to be served on the face of the earth. The apostles were there at the personal invitation of Jesus. Likewise, Jesus invites each of us individually to his Eucharistic banquet. In our Baptism he gave us a share in his priestly power. He invites us to join him in offering our praise and thanks to the Father. Can you imagine the excitement and anticipation the apostles must have felt? Even though the hatred and intrigue was increasing around them, the apostles must have noticed that Jesus was eager to eat this Passover meal with them. As they took their places at the table, their eyes must have been fixed on Jesus during the whole meal. (Take your place at the table and listen.)

Colloquy: Jesus, how grateful I am that you have invited me to join you daily at your Eucharistic banquet. The privilege is too much for my mind to fathom. Touch me with your love that I may be drawn more deeply into its significance.

THIRD REFLECTION

v. 15 "I have greatly desired to eat this Passover with you before I suffer."

The heart of Jesus must have been filled with mixed emotions. He realized that this was going to be his last meal with his dearest friends, yet he was filled with exhilaration and excitement about what he was going to do for them. He had been anticipating this meal. He had prepared the apostles by proving his power over wine at Cana and his power over bread in Galilee. Was their faith strong enough to accept this great gift of himself hidden under the simple elements of bread and wine? No matter, he was going to give them the gift and the Holy Spirit would eventually lead them to an understanding of the "breaking of the bread." (Sit quietly in the Upper Room and listen.)

Colloquy: Lord Jesus, you greatly desire to eat this Passover meal with me daily. Each day I have the privilege of offering the Eucharist with you. I need to be reminded of the great privilege which is mine. Thank you for your goodness to me.

FOURTH REFLECTION

v. 19 "Then taking bread and giving thanks, he broke it and gave it to them saying: 'This is my body to be given for you.' "

Jesus did four important things in this brief statement. He *took*, he *blessed*, he *broke*, he *gave*. Jesus *took* the bread, a simple, ordinary gift. He calls us simple, ordinary people to be his special friends. He *blessed* the bread to set it aside for God's use only. Jesus blesses us by calling us into discipleship, by setting us apart for his work and as his instrument of love and peace. Jesus

147

broke the bread. In order to become disciples of Jesus we need to be formed and transformed. This requires some breaking. Finally Jesus *gave*. He gave us himself as a very special gift to nourish, strengthen, and above all to live with us and to love us. Jesus became Eucharist for us. He fills us with himself and then asks us to become Eucharist to others. That is the import of the dismissal at Mass: "Go in peace to love and serve the Lord." (Let Jesus take, bless, break and give to you.)

Colloquy: Jesus, what a privilege to be called into a covenant agreement with you. How gracious of you to come to me. How kind of you to entrust me to become Eucharist to others. Be with me to help me.

FIFTH REFLECTION

v. 19 "This is my body to be given for you."

With this brief statement a great miracle took place, so great was the power of his Word. Simple, ordinary bread became the body and blood of Jesus. Jesus is Eucharistically present under the species of bread and wine. How accommodating Jesus is. Jesus wanted to remain with us and within us. He could have done so in countless different ways. However, he knew how difficult it would be for us to grasp his spiritual presence only; hence he gave us this visible sign of his presence. His tangible presence under the appearance of bread is also significant because he came to nourish and strengthen us for our pilgrimage through life. His visible presence does require faith. This acceptance of him in faith and trust is very pleasing to him. ("My Lord and my God!")

Colloquy: Jesus, I do believe, help my unbelief. Thank you for your Eucharistic presence within me. Thank you for the great privilege of coming to you daily to meet you, to be nourished and fed by you, but especially to be loved by you. I love you too.

148

SIXTH REFLECTION

v. 20 "He did the same with the cup after eating, saying as he did so: 'This cup is the new covenant in my blood, which will be shed for you'."

Jesus gave us himself under these two species—bread and wine—to assure us of his complete and entire presence with us. He also did so to help us understand the sacrificial nature of his Eucharistic presence. He continues to purify, sanctify and unite himself with us in the Eucharistic sacrifice. At the Last Supper, Jesus consecrated the third cup required at the Passover meal, the cup of thanksgiving. How appropriate is this cup of thanksgiving for this tremendous gift of the transcendent God of heaven and earth making himself so immanent to us that we dare to come without fear or trepidation to receive him as our spiritual food. What a joyous reminder that he continues to cleanse us by the power of his precious blood. All we say is "God is love." (Be present to him and let him speak to you.)

Colloquy: Jesus, the wonder of it all makes me exclaim with St. Paul: "How deep are the riches and the wisdom and the knowledge of God! How inscrutable his judgments, how unsearchable his ways!" As my heart is filled with a sense of your presence all I can do is respond with "Thank you for loving me. I love you too."

SEVENTH REFLECTION

v. 19 "Do this as a remembrance of me."

Jesus' request is direct and imperative. He knew that we would soon forget. He also knew that we would need him every moment of the day. What greater privilege can we have. (Pause and listen to that hymn of praise rising heavenward at this moment.)

Colloquy: Lord Jesus, how can I fathom this mystery of your love? How can I understand a love so great that it wants to come to me eucharistically each day? It overwhelms me. Let my heart respond with all the love I am able to give.

If you wish to continue to contemplate this tremendous mystery of God's love, the following passages may be helpful:

John 13:1-17 — "If I do not wash you . . . you will have no share in my heritage."

I Corinthians 11:23-29 — "A man should examine himself first; only then should he eat of the bread and drink of the cup."

John 10:17-18 — "The Father loves me for this: that I lay down my life to take it up again."

Other accounts of the institution of the Holy Eucharist can be found in Matthew 26:20-30 and Mark 14:17-26.

23 Agony in the Garden

Loneliness Too Is Suffering
Matthew 26:36-46

Some years ago my grandmother became very ill and was hospitalized. When I went to visit her I discovered that she was too ill to communicate. My grandfather sat beside her bed and would frequently turn his gaze on her. Not a single word passed between them. Occasionally he would gently and tenderly lay his hand on hers. As I was getting ready to leave, my grandfather accompanied me to the door of her room, and as we spoke softly, his glance would return to my grandmother, his spouse of fifty-four years. As I walked down the corridor with tear-filled eyes, I thought of the tenderness, the devotion, the compassion expressed so lovingly in that wordless communication, that loving presence to each other. I thought of the pain in the heart of Jesus during his agony in the Garden. He longed for human consolation, but he had to face this crucial moment alone.

FIRST REFLECTION

v. 36 "Stay here while I go over there and pray."
Jesus always prayed before the important events in his life. Prayer is the "warp and woof" of his life. Only in prayer do we find the strength to know and fulfill the Father's will. Jesus also needed human consolation. He

invited his closest friends, his apostles, to pray with him. He wanted his three favorite apostles even closer to him. On previous occasions Peter, John and James were his prayer companions. Now he needed them more than ever, but they failed him at this critical hour in his earthly life. Jesus was denied all human consolation. Even his Father seemed far removed. He had to face this great crisis alone. How much we need sympathetic companionship in times of stress and suffering. Jesus knew loneliness in his "hour," consequently he never leaves us alone, but is with us always. (Be with Jesus in the Garden.)

Colloquy: Jesus, you invite me daily to spend an hour with you. I am not proud of my response, or rather my lack of response. How much you want to enrich my life if only I will give you that time. Lord, grant me the grace to hear your invitation and the generosity to want to give you an hour each day.

SECOND REFLECTION

v. 38 "My heart is nearly broken with sorrow. Remain here and stay awake with me."

Jesus wants his closest friends to "remain" with him. This is an ideal prayer posture. Prayer is not only addressing our words and thoughts to God. It is not only thinking about God and all his goodness. No, prayer is just "being for God" and letting him "be for us." Just to bask in the sunshine of his presence and let his love warm us, nourish us, encourage us, cheer us is real prayer. Prayer is longing for a deeper, more personal relationship with God our Father. Prayer is resting in his presence in wordless communication. ("Stay awake with me" . . . Jesus).

Colloquy: Thank you, Jesus, for inviting me to "remain" with you in this contemplative posture. Mold, shape, form and transform this heart of mine according to your mind. Let me stay with you always.

THIRD REFLECTION

v. 39 "My Father, if it is possible, let this cup pass me by. Still, let it be as you would have it, not as I."

Jesus wanted to spend this time in prayer so that he could hear at the very depth of his being what the Father was asking of him. Only after time spent in prayerful communication with his Father could Jesus say "as you will it, not as I." Time spent in prayer helps us to see everything through God's eyes. The Father gave Jesus the reassurance, the encouragement, the love which his human nature needed at that moment. Prayer leads us to the mountain top where our vision becomes more panoramic. Prayer melts away our own ideas and desires and makes us more receptive to what God wants. Time spent in prayer helps us to put on the mind of Jesus. It aids us in thinking, acting and reacting as Jesus would. (Look into Jesus' eyes as he says yes to the Father.)

Colloquy: Jesus, by your power and grace help me always and in every situation to say "as you would have it, not as I." Teach me that only in foregoing my own will and in giving myself to you will I find true joy.

FOURTH REFLECTION

v. 40 "So you could not stay awake with me for even an hour."

Jesus invited his friends to pray with him, to support him in his agony. He also knew that prayer would enable them to understand God's will and his divine plan in what was about to happen. Jesus knew that only in prayer could they comprehend the purpose of all the tragic events which were to follow in rapid succession. In prayer they would experience love without which they themselves would not be able to accept the Father's plan of salvation. Only the love experienced and augmented in prayer would give them the strength and power they needed to fulfill their role in these tragic but salvific events. (Spend the "hour" with Jesus.)

Colloquy: Jesus, you invite me to make a daily date with you. You invite me to stay awake with you for even an hour, so that I too can experience the Father's love. Thank you for your kind invitation. Only with your grace can I respond daily to your invitation. Grant me that gift.

FIFTH REFLECTION

v. 42 "My Father, if this cannot pass me by without my drinking it, your will be done!"

The principal concern of Jesus during his earthly sojourn was to do the will of the Father at all times and in the situations of every day. "I have come to do your will, O God" (*Hebrews 10:7*). His mission in life was to fulfill his Father's will exactly. To understand the importance of doing the Father's will, Jesus gave us a special Beatitude: "Blest are the single-hearted. . . ." (*Matthew 5:8*). If we are striving to do the Father's will, we will be better able to acquire that ideal prayer posture: "Here I am, Lord, what is it you want of me this day, this hour, this moment?" This attitude is the road to holiness. It is the source of genuine joy and happiness. This attitude brings us much peace. (Listen to Jesus accepting the Father's will.)

Colloquy: Jesus, how graciously you taught me the importance of keeping my will in tune with your will. Strengthen me to say yes at all times even when I experience rebellion within myself.

SIXTH REFLECTION

v. 45 "Sleep on now. Enjoy your rest!"

Jesus' words register the pain, sorrow and disappointment which was in his heart. Yet he understood the humanness of the apostles. How badly he needed their human support and consolation. How much com-

154

fort they might have brought him in this "his hour." These were his personal friends upon whom he depended to carry on his Church. Jesus was disappointed because he wanted them to discover in prayer the redemptive purpose of his sufferings and also to acquire the vision of the kingdom which he came to establish. Without this understanding it would be so difficult to fulfill the role to which they were called. The apostles too were disappointed in themselves. They loved Jesus deeply. They wanted to be with him, but their human nature failed them. They too must have had heavy hearts. Jesus loved them just the same. In fact, he asked the soldiers to take him, but to let "these" go their way. (Listen to what Jesus is saying to you.)

Colloquy: Jesus, you called me to a special mission in life. Thank you for calling me into discipleship. Thank you for the trust you place in me. Help me to spend sufficient time in prayer to enable me to see, understand and fulfill my role.

SEVENTH REFLECTION

v. 46 "Get up! Let us be on our way!"

The prayer of Jesus in the Garden of Gethsemane is important. In prayer Jesus found the strength and courage to fulfill the role to which the Father had called him. His agony was the most critical temptation with which Jesus was confronted. After spending time alone with his Father in prayer, he was able to acquiesce to his Father's will. Jesus invites us to "get up and be on our way" by calling us frequently to prayer. How many times in his Word are we asked to be alone with the Lord, to listen intently at the very core of our being, to pray without ceasing. This frequent call is not merely a duty. It is a means to help us fulfill our total role in the Father's plan. Prayer gives us vision, courage, strength and perseverance. Only then can we be "on our way." (Listen, listen, listen.)

Colloquy: Jesus, how eloquently you told me: "Apart from me you can do nothing." With you, in prayer, I can do all things. Thank you for being "with" me and "within" me always.

To continue your prayer on this theme of struggle, we suggest the following passages:

Matthew 4:1-11	"Then Jesus was led into the desert by the Spirit to be tempted by the devil."
Luke 22:31-38	"Remember that Satan has asked for you, to sift you all like wheat."
Hebrews 2:1-18	"Since he was himself tested through what he suffered, he is able to help those who are tempted."
Hebrews 5:1-10	"He offered prayers and supplications with loud cries and tears to God . . . ."
II Corinthians 1:3-7	"He comforts us in all our afflictions. . . ."

24 The Passion of Jesus

Test, Temptation, Trial
Luke 22:47-71

The cross of Jesus is mystery at its depths. How can we understand a God who becomes a victim of his wicked and whimsical creatures? How can we understand the mind of Jesus who "humbled himself, obediently accepting even death, death on a cross"? How can we fathom the depth of the heart of Jesus who said: "I lay down my life to take it up again. No one takes it from me; I lay it down freely." Jesus himself gives us the only plausible explanation: "There is no greater love than this: to lay down one's life for one's friends." Live that mystery with Jesus in prayer and strive to plumb the depths of that love.

FIRST REFLECTION

v. 48 "Judas, would you betray the Son of Man with a kiss?"

What a tragic hour for Jesus! He was experiencing the dreadful pain of rejection and the anticipation of the great suffering which awaited him. Added to all this was the traitorous treachery of one of his own apostles. Even though this was a very dark hour for Jesus, he towered majestically above all the perfidy. He did not threaten Judas, but made one final gesture of love to him: "Judas, would you betray the Son of Man with a kiss?" (Listen to Jesus' heart as he faces Judas.)

Colloquy: Jesus, when human weakness, anger, fear and temptation beset me let me hear those pleading words spoken in love to me: "Would you betray the Son of Man with a kiss?" Thank you, Jesus, for showing me how to reach out in love even in moments of betrayal.

SECOND REFLECTION

v. 53 "This is your hour—the triumph of darkness!"

Jesus is always king and conqueror, but evil had to have its hour so that his almighty power might shine forth. This was the hour of evil, and what a sorrowful hour for Jesus. In spite of apparent victory for evil, Jesus was still the conqueror. He assured us: "I lay down my life . . . No one takes it from me; I lay it down freely. I have power to lay it down and I have power to take it up again" (*John* 10:17). By his immolation on the cross he conquered sin and death. Yes, Jesus loved us so much that he could not do anything short of giving himself totally and entirely. By his death and resurrection he was able to share his divine life with us even in this land of exile. (Stay very close to Jesus. Give him the assurance of your presence.)

Colloquy: Jesus, your great love for me must win a loving response from me. You gave your life for my salvation. Grant me the grace to give myself eagerly and generously, even though my heart is so timid.

THIRD REFLECTION

vv. 57-60 "Woman, I do not know him."

What a dichotomy in Peter. He loved Jesus so very much. He wanted to be close to him not only out of curiosity to see what was going to happen to Jesus, but also to support and defend him if possible. Yes, Peter knew the fate which could be his as a follower of Jesus. He might be arrested and accused and ultimately put to death with Jesus. Fear and panic gripped him for a moment and won the battle even before Peter had time to think. It is true that we react to our subconscious habit patterns. Peter was not yet fully imbued with a sense of mission regardless of the price; hence, the sudden denial to protect himself. Peter could not believe his own ears. (Listen to your own words on some past occasion.)

Colloquy: Lord Jesus, I do love you. I want to be loyal to you. I want to serve you faithfully, but I know how weak I am. I am so likely to deny you as Peter did. I need you to continue to remind me of my weakness and to rescue me in time of crisis.

FOURTH REFLECTION

v. 61 "The Lord turned around and looked at Peter, and Peter remembered the word that the Lord had spoken to him. . . ."

How piercing must have been the eyes of Jesus. How deeply they reached into Peter's soul. Yet it was not a look of reproach, nor of condemnation, but a loving appeal to Peter to help him realize what he had done. What guilt, what regret, what sorrow must have welled up in Peter's heart, yet there was no remorse. He immediately recognized his weakness, his failure, his sinfulness. On many occasions during Jesus' public ministry, Peter witnessed Jesus reaching out to others with a forgiving, healing love. He knew that Jesus would forgive his weakness as he had done on so many previous occasions. Jesus knew that there was no malice in Peter's denial. It was human weakness. How often in moments of fear of rejection of or criticism, I have denied Jesus in the same way! (Let the eyes of Jesus search your soul.)

Colloquy: Jesus, I have failed you over and over again. How often I denied you! Please do not turn your eyes away from me, lest I fall even more gravely. Let me turn to you in sorrow, as soon as I fall, without making excuses. May remorse never take possession of me.

FIFTH REFLECTION

vv. 63-65 "Meanwhile the men guarding Jesus amused themselves at his expense."

Pause for a moment to recall what is taking place. The transcendent God of heaven and earth is being slapped, taunted, ridiculed, insulted by his own creatures, even though their next heartbeat depends upon his goodness to them. His providential love is sustaining life in them at this very moment, yet they dare to strike him. Love enfolds so many mysteries. How aptly the prophet quoted God as saying: "I will not give vent to my blazing anger . . . for I am God and not man, the Holy One present among you" (*Hosea 11:9*). (Listen to each insult as it stings the heart of Jesus.)

Colloquy: Jesus, thank you for being so gracious and gentle with me when I was so indifferent to your love, even when I dared to say no to your love. Please accept my love in atonement for the abuse you had to suffer for my sake.

SIXTH REFLECTION

v. 69 "From now on, the Son of Man will have his seat at the right hand of the power of God."

Jesus repeatedly spoke of the necessity of suffering in order to fulfill his role as the Son of Man. He also said that his suffering was his glorification. Because of his obedient suffering, he is in his glory sending the Holy Spirit to sanctify us. "The Lord said to my Lord: 'Sit at my right hand till I make your enemies your footstool' " (*Psalm 110:1*). St. Peter set forth this same truth in his very first sermon: "Exalted at God's right hand, he first received the promised Holy Spirit from the Father, then poured this Spirit out on us" (*Acts 2:33*). St. Stephen, the first martyr, testified to the same truth: "Stephen meanwhile, filled with the Holy Spirit, looked to the sky above and saw the glory of God, and Jesus standing at God's right hand" (*Acts 7:55*). (Ponder the work of redemption going on within you.)

Colloquy: Jesus, your glory is your redemptive work being wrought in me at every moment of the day. Help me to be open and receptive to your powerful influence. Thank you for redeeming me.

SEVENTH REFLECTION

v. 71 "What need have we of witnesses?"

How correctly did his enemies say that they had no need of witnesses. They had already decided on his guilt and his fate: death by crucifixion. Witnesses would only complicate matters. What perfidy, what hypocrisy, what injustice in this ridiculous mock trial! "More tortuous than all else is the human heart, beyond remedy; who can understand it? I, the Lord, alone probe the mind and test the heart" (*Jeremiah* 17:9f). Against such intrigue Jesus never attempted to defend himself. He was silent. What heroic humility! (Look at my own heart.)

Colloquy: Jesus, what a noble example you gave me! How do I react when I am criticized, accused. Do I threaten revenge? Do I let resentment ruin my peace of mind and heart? Let me learn from your example.

To continue your prayer on the sufferings of Jesus we would suggest: (Any part of the passion from any one of the Gospels.)

Isaiah 52:13 to 53:12	The Suffering Servant
Galatians 3:1-14	". . . before whose eyes Jesus Christ was displayed to view upon his cross . . . ."
Galatians 6:11-18	"May I never boast of anything but the cross of our Lord Jesus Christ!"

25 The Death of Jesus

O My People, What Have I Done To You?
John 19:17-30

The moments of death are solemn and sober moments, but they are sanctified by a mysterious presence radiating peace. These moments are precious because the last acts or words of a person are treasured. How often has the dying wish of a parent or spouse changed the whole course of another's life? The final words are treasured by every Christian. Revisit Calvary. Remain there. Listen to the mockery, the derision, the blasphemy, the insults, yet hear the voice of Jesus rising far above onslaught of hatred as he prays: "Father, forgive them; they do not know what they are doing."

FIRST REFLECTION

v. 18 "There they crucified him, and two others with
    him; one on either side, Jesus in the middle."
Death by crucifixion was the most shameful kind of execution known in those days. It brought dishonor and disgrace to the whole family of the criminal and all his descendants. It was also the most painful kind of death since life gradually ebbed away and ultimately the person became too weak to hold up his head to breathe, and often died of suffocation. Jesus freely laid down his life. He accepted this ignominious death in order to prove the depth of his love for us. He loved us

so much he had to give everything down to the last drop of his blood. There could be no doubt about the immensity of his love. What an overwhelming love! (Visit Calvary. Stay there and let the impact of the event fill your whole being.)

Colloquy: Jesus, you ask me to take up my cross daily and follow in your footsteps. How I hesitate! Sometimes my cross seems dreadfully heavy, and sometimes—dare I say it—unfair. Fill me with your love so that I can joyfully give without counting the cost.

SECOND REFLECTION

v. 19 "Jesus the Nazorean, the King of the Jews."

Jesus is a king! He is my king, my Lord. Jesus said to Pilate: "My kingdom does not belong to this world." The kingdom which Jesus came to establish is a kingdom of love. Love is its unifying power. In fact, love alone can unite us in a Christian community. Love makes us brothers and sisters to one another. This is the kingdom which Jesus came to establish among us. He is our king because he is the source of love in our lives. He tells us: "As the Father has loved me, so I have loved you," and that means he loves us with an infinite love. Again he reminds us how much he loves us when he says: "There is no greater love than this: to lay down one's life for one's friends" (*John 15:9 & 13*). By his voluntary death on the cross Jesus proved his infinite love for us. By his resurrection from the dead, he is able to share his divine life and love with us by living within us. Surely, "there is no greater love than this. . . ." (Be still and experience Jesus' divine life surging through your whole being.)

Colloquy: Jesus, you are asking me to let you fill me with your divine love so that you can reach out to others in love through me. Help me dispose of all the debris so that I can be a channel of your love to others.

THIRD REFLECTION

v. 23 "After the soldiers had crucified Jesus they took his garments and divided them four ways, one for each soldier."

Jesus wanted to give everything as a total response in love. He was born in a "borrowed" cave. He could say: "The Son of Man has nowhere to lay his head." On Calvary he was deprived of everything. He was dispossessed even of the garments he was wearing. Tradition tells us that the seamless tunic might have been the work of his Mother. Even this treasure had to be disposed of. No keepsakes, no heirlooms, nothing was to be withheld. Every attachment had to be broken, if he was to make a total gift of himself. (Strive to free your heart from every attachment.)

Colloquy: Jesus, you know my weak human nature and how attached I am. My greatest attachment is my own selfish will. Free me from all the inordinate attachments which rob me of the joy and freedom you want me to have. Let me experience the happiness of total detachment.

FOURTH REFLECTION

v. 25 "Near the cross of Jesus there stood his mother. . . ."

Without an adjective and without an adverb, John describes Mary's complete oblation of herself in union with the redemptive work of her Son. John's single statement is a short, short story of utter pathos, total oblation and loving immolation. Mary had given her *fiat* without reservation and she was determined to be faithful to that commitment to the very end. Filled with love she united her sufferings along with the excruciating pain of her Son. Mary was sinless which meant that she understood more keenly the bitter pain of rejection of her Son. She loved her own people and knew what suffering their rejection would bring them. Through all this Mary "stood" near the cross. She did not scream out at the injustice. She did not threaten. She did not call upon the Father to punish the blasphemers and the executioners. Mary "stood." (Welcome Mary as your Mother.)

Colloquy: Jesus, you gave me your Mother as a model of total dedication. Mary, teach me to be generous and faithful in all the mysterious events of my life. Obtain for me that grace always to want the Father's will in everything that happens to me in life.

FIFTH REFLECTION

vv. 26-27 "There is your son . . . There is your mother."

Jesus lavished his gifts upon us throughout his earthly life. In death he gave us a unique treasure—his Mother as our very own mother. How aptly the Fathers of Vatican Council II called Mary the "Mother of the Church." She is, in every sense of the word, the Mother of the family of God. As our Mother, Mary is vitally concerned about us. She does not want a single drop of the Precious Blood of her Son to be poured out in vain. As Mother of the Church Mary, along with her Son, our Mediator before the Father, intercedes with the whole Church before the throne of God. She begs that all persons, including ourselves, come to the eternal union with the Father. How earnestly the Church prays: "Never was it known on earth that anyone who implored your help or sought your intercession was left unaided." (Thank Jesus for the gift of his Mother.)

Colloquy: Lord Jesus, you showered all these fruits upon me when you invited me through Baptism to become a member of your family. Your Father became my Abba and your Mother became my Mother. "Holy Mary, Mother of God, pray for us sinners now and at the hour of our death."

v. 28 "After that, Jesus, realizing that everything was now finished, said to fulfill the Scripture, 'I am thirsty.' "

How the heart of Jesus thirsted! How he longed for souls! How he wanted to draw all men, even his enemies into the warmth of his love. "How often have I yearned to gather your children, as a mother bird gathers her young under her wings, but you refused me" (*Matthew 23:37*). Love wants to be closely united with the person loved. Jesus wanted to bring the consolations of peace and joy to those who hated him, to those who were indifferent to him, to those who hesitated to accept him. He said: "I came that they might have life and have it to the full" (*John 10:10*). What anguish in the sad fact: "To his own he came, yet his own did not accept him" (*John 1:11*). What a plaintive cry; "I am thirsty." (Experience the parchness of Jesus' thirst.)

Colloquy: Jesus, what hope, what joy, you give me through your Word: "Anyone who did accept him, he empowered to become children of God." Thank you for empowering me. Grant me the grace to make my acceptance more generous each day.

SEVENTH REFLECTION

v. 30 "Then he bowed his head, and delivered over his spirit."

Jesus promised us that he would not leave us orphans, but that he would remain with us always. Yes, "He had loved his own in this world, and would show his love for them to the end" (*John 13:1*). Jesus had accomplished his redemptive work, now the fruit of that redemption must be applied to each one of us. From his pierced side the Church was born. "Of his fullness we have all had a share—love following upon love" (*John 1:16*). The Word became flesh and made his dwelling among us . . . filled with enduring love" (*John 1:14*). Now Jesus was not going to leave us, but would remain with us and within us. He was going to send us his Spirit. "I will ask the Father and he will give you another Paraclete—to be with you always: the Spirit of truth . . . you can recognize him because he remains with you and will be within you" (*John 14:16*). (Let the Spirit reveal his presence within you.)

Colloquy: Yes, Jesus you did love your own until the end, and you do love me and will continue to love me regardless of what I do. Draw me more and more into an understanding of that mystery of your love so that I may respond in greater love to you. Never let me sever the bond of love.

To continue this theme of prayer, listen to Jesus as he speaks from the throne of his cross:

Matthew 27:46	"My God, my God, why have you forsaken me?"
Luke 23:34	"Father, forgive them; they do not know what they are doing."
Luke 23:43	"I assure you: this day you will be with me in paradise."
Luke 23:46	"Father, into your hands I recommend my spirit."
John 19:28	"I am thirsty"
John 19:26 & 27	"Woman, there is your son . . . . There is your mother."
John 19:30	"Now it is finished."

26 Appearances to the Disciples

"My Lord And My God"
John 20:19-29

Long before his incarnation into our world, Jesus
was announced by the Prophet as the "Prince of
Peace." He came into the world "to guide our feet into
the way of peace." Jesus also told us: "Peace is my
farewell to you, my peace is my gift to you." Jesus gave
us his Holy Spirit and "the fruit of the spirit is love, joy,
peace." Peace is more than a feeling. It is more than a
condition. Peace springs from a close, personal relationship with Jesus. It arises from our fundamental
option to serve Jesus as faithfully as we can by keeping
ourselves as free from sin as possible. How many
times, especially after his resurrection, does Jesus ex-
tend this blessing to us: "Peace be with you." He gave
us the Sacrament of Reconciliation so that he could
come to us personally and individually either to restore
or to maintain that peace-filled relationship with us.
Peace is our foretaste of heaven.

FIRST REFLECTION

v. 19 "Jesus came and stood before them. 'Peace be
with you'," he said.

Even though the doors were locked Jesus came and
stood before the apostles. Jesus was present with them
all the time. They could not see him until he revealed
his presence. Jesus was present with them already in

his resurrected life. He is continually present with us even though we cannot see him. He is spirit. Just as our room is filled with radio and television signals, yet we cannot hear or see the picture until we have the proper receiving set. Our physical bodies are not capable of seeing Jesus or hearing him, yet he is more present to us than all the radio and television signals, even more present than we are to ourselves. At Baptism Jesus blessed us with his divine life. He will never leave us. His presence and his power within us makes us Christians. His presence is the source of our peace. "Peace is my farewell to you, my peace is my gift to you." Peace is more than an experience or a feeling. It brings joy in this life and salvation in the life to come. How frequently Jesus greets us with: "Peace be with you." (Contemplate the risen Jesus living within you.)

Colloquy: Lord Jesus, I know that you are living with me and within me. Bless me in such a way that I may more readily be aware of your indwelling and your abiding presence. Teach me how to recognize you in all those you send across my path each day. Fill me with your peace.

SECOND REFLECTION

v. 20 "At the sight of the Lord the disciples rejoiced."

Imagine the consternation, but also the joy which the sudden presence of Jesus meant to the apostles. His presence was a complete surprise because as yet they did not understand the scriptures—that Jesus was going to rise from the dead. Our faith gives us the assurance that Jesus is present with us in his resurrected life. Like the apostles we are so pragmatic. We need constant reassurances. "He (Jesus) showed them his hands and his side." We too need signs and proofs. Our limited minds are so slow to grasp the divine. Jesus gave us many outward signs to help us accept his divine presence. These signs are not always totally obvious. They require some faith and our faith-response pleases Jesus. Some of these signs are the sacraments which Jesus gave us to purify, sanctify and strengthen us along the highway of life. How gracious of Jesus to adapt himself to our human limitations. (Let Jesus show you his hands and his side.)

Colloquy: With the apostles, Jesus, let me always rejoice in your presence in my life. Keep me ever aware of your abiding presence so that I may respond more fully to your love. Let my thoughts carry on a continuous conversation with you.

THIRD REFLECTION

v. 21 "As the Father has sent me, so I send you."

To be an apostle we must be formally sent. Jesus was sent by the Father. Now in turn he was sending his own apostles. He conferred his divine power upon them, then he commissioned them to go forth in his name. There are three stages involved in apostleship. Jesus first called the apostles to follow him. Next he conditioned them by means of a three-year-program so that they might understand something about his way of life and that they might have his mind. Finally he asked for their commitment and then he sent them into his vineyard. Jesus calls each one of us to some kind of apostolate as we strive to live out our baptismal commitment. We too need conditioning so that we may have the mind of Jesus. Jesus asks for our commitment to whatever he may call us. Only love can be the power which helps us to commit ourselves, like Mary, without reservation. (Reflect on your special call from Jesus.)

Colloquy: Thank you, Lord, for calling me by name. Teach me now to submit eagerly to the conditioning necessary to make my thinking like yours, then empower me to commit myself totally to you.

FOURTH REFLECTION

vv. 22-23 "Receive the Holy Spirit. If you forgive
men's sins, they are forgiven them. . . ."

Jesus paid the penalty of our sins by his sacrificial
death on the cross. The Holy Spirit, the Sanctifier, is
now carrying out the work of purification and sanctifi-
cation in all of us. Jesus died for our sins; they are
pardoned and forgiven, but this forgiveness seems to
be so impersonal, so universal. Jesus wanted to assure
us personally and individually of his forgiving, healing
love. He instituted the Sacrament of Reconciliation in
which he comes to us personally to assure us that he is
forgiving and healing us. We encounter him personally
in all the sacraments. What a joy to meet him personally to receive his forgiveness and healing. What loving
and gracious concern for each one of us. (Let the truth
of Jesus' presence in the sacraments reassure your
heart.)

Colloquy: Jesus, how graciously you have taken into
consideration all my human weaknesses and how
generously you have provided for all my needs. Keep
me aware of your presence in all the sacraments. Teach
me to show my gratitude by using well your precious
gift of the Sacrament of Reconciliation.

FIFTH REFLECTION

v. 25 "I will never believe it without probing the nail-
prints in his hands, without putting my finger in
the nailmarks and my hand into his side."

Thomas wanted to believe, but he was afraid. So
many things had happened the last few days which
shattered him. He knew that Jesus died in utter disgrace. He wanted Jesus to be alive, but how could he be
sure that the other apostles were not deluded? They too
loved Jesus and they could be suffering hallucinations.
Thomas wanted to believe, but he was afraid it might
not be true. He could not comprehend how Jesus, who

had just died such a dreadful death, could be alive and well. How often we utter these words of Thomas and with little variation! How often our pride and skepticism gets into the way of faith! How often we ask for proof! Faith is making a leap into the dark, and yet it is not so much a leap into the dark as a leap into our Father's arms. (Say to Jesus: "I believe.")

Colloquy: Jesus, you know that I want to believe. I want to recognize your divine plan in every event of my daily life, but how fearful I am. How skeptical! Please give me a deep, abiding, operative faith. Teach me that the only way I can have a strong faith is simply to step out in faith daily.

SIXTH REFLECTION

v. 26 "A week later, the disciples were once more in the room, and this time Thomas was with them . . . . Jesus came and stood before them."

Jesus teaches us another delightful facet of his personality. How patient he was with Thomas. He came again to show his loving concern for him. Jesus graciously and humbly submitted to Thomas' demands. Even though he is the God of heaven and earth, Jesus often accommodates himself to our human weakness and needs. He wants to win our faith and love. How often, because of our weak faith, we demand a sign from Jesus! Jesus willingly gives us that sign provided we are open to receive it. Jesus asked Thomas to verify for himself that he was alive. He asked Thomas to: "Take your finger and examine my hands. Put your hand into my side." Then Jesus gives us and Thomas that great admonition: "Do not persist in your unbelief, but believe!" (Hold Jesus' hands in yours and look at his wounds.)

Colloquy: Jesus, how bold I am to lay a fleece before you so often. I am ashamed of my weak and doubting faith on so many occasions. How frequently you have proved your great power and concern in my life and yet I continue to doubt. Thank you for acquiescing to my demands even though you are God. Forgive my lack of faith.

SEVENTH REFLECTION

v. 28 "My Lord and my God!"

What a loving response, what a submissive response to the persuasive power of Jesus. Thomas doubted, but his obstinacy melted before the loving consideration of Jesus. What a tremendous act of faith! Unequivocally Thomas called Jesus—God. This is the first time that any apostle spoke out so forcefully. "My Lord and my God!" How pleased Jesus must have been with this public act of faith. How many times has this act of faith poured out of the hearts of people the world over. "My Lord and my God!" Jesus also used this occasion to impart a lesson on faith: "You became a believer because you saw me. Blest are they who have not seen and have believed." May we be blest because of our faith. (Let your heart say: "I believe.")

Colloquy: Thank you, Jesus, for permitting Thomas' act of faith to re-echo throughout the centuries. What a valuable lesson you have taught me in dealing with Thomas. Please be gentle with my lack of faith. Help me to say, and always mean it when I say: "My Lord and my God!"

Pray often with this theme of faith. It will help you live in his presence and experience his love. Here are a few suggestions:

John 4:46-50	"Unless you people see signs and wonders, you do not believe."
Luke 1:39-45	"Blest is she who trusted that the Lord's words to her would be fulfilled."
Mark 2:1-12	"When Jesus saw their faith . . . My son, your sins are forgiven."

| John 14:1-14 | "Have faith in God and faith in me." |
| John 11:1-44 | "Do you believe this?" |

27 Road to Emmaus

An Awareness Walk
Luke 24:13-35

One of our modern hymns has the lyrical refrain "Lord Jesus, you shall be our song as we journey." How aptly this describes our daily trek to Emmaus. We have all enjoyed a leisurely walk in the country or in a city park with the flowers in full bloom, the trees lifting their branches up in prayer and the birds singing their praises to the Lord. At such times and in such settings God seems so very close to us. We can almost feel his presence in his creative beauty around us. Jesus gives us the assurance that each day he walks with us, experiences our fears and frustrations and rejoices in our fun and frolicking. We must continually remind ourselves of his abiding presence so that our whole life may be an awareness walk with Jesus.

FIRST REFLECTION

v. 15 "In the course of their lively exchange, Jesus approached and began to walk along with them."

Each day we make our own journey to our own Emmaus. It may be our daily trip to work, or even just around home performing the many household duties. Jesus told us that he would remain "with" us and "within" us through the indwelling of the Holy Spirit. We are never alone as we go about the business of daily living. Jesus is always with us. He is more real to us than he was to the disciples before the Resurrection. He is more present than the oxygen we breathe or the blood circulating through our veins. (Let your heart speak to Jesus within you.)

Colloquy: Jesus, I believe you are present here. I acknowledge your presence. Help me to communicate with you constantly throughout this day by thanking you, by asking your help and advice and above all by loving you and permitting you to love me.

SECOND REFLECTION

v. 25 "What little sense you have!"

Jesus wanted to jar the disciples out of their state of disappointment and discouragement and turn their thoughts to the real significance of his suffering and death. He wanted them to focus their attention to the possibility that what happened might be in God's plan. His words: "What little sense you have," did just that. These words of Jesus remind us of the Penitential Rite of the Mass. Jesus recalled their incredulity in order to have them grow in faith. At Mass we recall our faults and failures in order to recognize our need for redemption and to seek it through the Eucharistic sacrifice. (Reflect on God's plan in your life.)

Colloquy: Jesus, how slow I am to believe. With the father of the possessed boy I say: "I do believe! Help my lack of trust!" Walk with me that I may imitate your mind.

THIRD REFLECTION

v. 27 "Beginning, then, with Moses and all the prophets, he interpreted for them every passage of Scripture which referred to him."

Jesus showed his disciples the meaning of the Scriptures. All that happened to him was prophesied and fulfilled as the Father had predetermined. Only with this understanding did the tragic events of his passion and death make sense. Each day Jesus opens the Scriptures for us in the Liturgy of the Word. In fact Vatican Council II tells us that when the Scriptures are read in Church, it is Christ himself who is speaking to us. In his Word Jesus gives us the inspiration and motivation which we need each day. Only in the light of his Word does the jigsaw puzzle of life make sense. (Listen attentively to his Word.)

Colloquy: Jesus, give me a quiet, listening heart as you open your Word for me in prayer. As I come to the table of your Word each day may it nourish, inspire and encourage me. Give me a listening heart.

FOURTH REFLECTION

v. 29 " 'Stay with us. It is nearly evening—the day is practically over.' So he went in to stay with them."

Jesus respects our free will. It is his gift to us and he regards it as something very sacred. He does not intrude, rather he spends much time waiting. Only when the disciples invited him, did Jesus stay with them.

Only when they became receptive to him did he reveal himself to them. When we come to him in prayer, and only when we invite him to come to us, does he reveal his presence to us. It may be a sense of awe and reverence, an outpouring of his love, an enjoyment of his peace. (Ask Jesus to stay with you.)

Colloquy: Jesus, make me receptive. I do invite you to come and stay with me. Help me to remove all the neon gods which replace you so many times in my life.

FIFTH REFLECTION

v. 30 "When he had seated himself with them to eat, he took bread, pronounced the blessing, then broke the bread and began to distribute it to them."

These four verbs speak eloquently to us. Jesus "took," "blessed," "broke" and "gave." Thus he gives himself to us each day. He comes to us so that he can call us into discipleship with him. He takes by inviting us to follow him. He blesses our ministry. He breaks by conditioning and converting us to his way of thinking and finally he wants us to give ourselves to him and to our brothers and sisters. Jesus becomes Eucharist for us so that we, in turn, can become Eucharist for others. (Let Jesus take, bless, break and give to you.)

Colloquy: Eucharistic Lord, draw me ever more deeply into the mystery of your love, so that I can respond in love to the apostolate to which you are calling me. Teach me not only to follow you, but to identify with you.

SIXTH REFLECTION

v. 32 "Were not our hearts burning inside us as he talked to us on the road and explained the Scriptures to us?"

God's Word is a powerful word. Like the rain and snow which goes forth and does not return until it has done its work, so God's Word does not return to him void, "but shall do my will, achieving the end for which I sent it." Jesus speaks his Word to us each day. Each day it is born again in our lives to inspire us, to convert us, to purify us, to transform us. Through his Word Jesus tells us who he is. We cannot know Jesus except by what he tells us about himself. Only when we know him in this way, can we love him. We cannot love someone we do not know. (Let his Word touch your heart.)

Colloquy: Jesus, keep revealing your Word to me, keep my heart ever burning within me, so that I really know you and commit myself to you without reservation.

v. 33 "They got up immediately and returned to
        Jerusalem, where they found the Eleven and the
        rest of the company assembled."

This reaction of the disciples must have been very
pleasing to Jesus. They had just come from Jerusalem,
the day was far spent, they were tired, yet they returned immediately to bring the good news to the rest
of the community. This loving concern to share the
good news is our apostolate. Jesus said: "Go, therefore,
and make disciples of all the nations . . . . And know
that I am with you always, until the end of the world!"
(*Matt. 28:19-20*). Jesus wants us to bring the joy which
only he can give to the entire world. He wants us to be
apostles of joy to a world which does not experience
this joy. That is our mission. (Rest quietly while he fills
you with his joy.)

Colloquy: Lord Jesus, permit me to be a channel of
your peace, your joy and your love to the world in
which you have placed me. Thank you for the Eucharistic joy which you give so graciously and so generously.

The following suggestions may help you walk more
closely with Jesus each day:

I John 1:1-3   "What we have seen with our
                       eyes . . . ."

I Peter 1:3-10   "Although you have never seen
                       him, you love him . . . ."

Song of Songs 3:1-5   "I found him whom my heart
                       loves."

28 Jesus Appears in Galilee

Picnic On The Shore
John 21:1-19

Jesus appeared to his apostles in their home environment along the Sea of Galilee. They loved the Sea. They were fishermen at heart. Jesus first met them here along the Lake and called them to follow him. At first he called them to travel with him, to listen to his teachings, to learn his attitudes, to absorb his mentality. They were passively receiving from him. Now Jesus called them to another stage of their apostolate. This time he asked for a fuller commitment. He commissioned them to "go and make disciples of all the nations." He appointed Peter the chief shepherd of his flock with the order: "Feed my lambs. Tend my sheep. Feed my sheep." They responded wholeheartedly to that call. They literally gave their lives. Jesus calls each one of us to follow him. As our vocation unfolds, he is asking us for an ongoing, fuller commitment. Therein we will find peace and happiness.

FIRST REFLECTION

v. 3 "Simon Peter said to them, 'I am going out to fish.' . . . All through the night they caught nothing."

The apostles returned to their home in Galilee. They went back to their former occupation, perhaps to support themselves for the moment. The statement "All through the night they caught nothing," could lend itself to several conclusions. Perhaps the Lord was trying to tell them in a different way that of themselves they could do nothing. They needed Jesus to be with them. Perhaps the Lord was also confirming the fact that they were no longer to ply their fishermen's trade, but to give themselves full time to preaching the good news. In our prayerful reflection we can draw other inferences. Be with the apostles in the boat. Listen to their conversation throughout the night. Did their conversation recall the first time they met Jesus as they returned from fishing? Were they regretting that Jesus was not with them now since on that occasion they had caught such a huge quantity of fish at his suggestion? (Be with the apostles and try to capture their loneliness without Jesus.)

Colloquy: Lord Jesus, only you can make all my efforts bear fruit. How often I catch nothing because I have tried to do things on my own. Remind me often of your words: "Apart from me you can do nothing."

SECOND REFLECTION

v. 6 " 'Cast your net off to the starboard side,' he suggested, 'and you will find something.' "

From his position on the shore Jesus might have been able to see a school of fish which the apostles could not see from the boat. That is one possible explanation. Secondly, Jesus wanted to reveal his identity gradually and therefore manifested his divine foreknowledge. The starboard side was always considered to be the lucky side of the boat for fishing. Jesus loved these men intensely. He did not want to see all their efforts bear no fruit. Perhaps they and their families had little to eat. Jesus, in his loving concern, came to their rescue. Jesus is very gentle and very sensitive to our free will. He does not force himself upon us. It was only when the apostles responded to his suggestion that they caught this huge number of fish. Only when we are receptive and obedient can Jesus work in us. (Listen to Jesus as he tries to guide you.)

Colloquy: Lord Jesus, you want to guide and help me in so many areas. Unfortunately I am so intoxicated with my own efficiency and ability I do not always hear you, nor do I come first to you to ask your help and inspiration. Thank you for your patience with me.

THIRD REFLECTION

v. 9 & 12 "When they landed, they saw a charcoal fire there with a fish laid on it and some bread . . . . 'Come and eat your meal,' Jesus told them."

Jesus knew that the apostles must have been hungry after laboring all night and having taken in nothing. They must have been disappointed, and maybe even discouraged. They were eager for any kindness shown them. Once again Jesus proves his loving concern. Did he not tell us that his Father cares for all the birds of the air and the lilies of the field? Did he not say that we are much more important than the sparrows? Jesus also knew that their hearts must have been heavy and confused as to the course of their lives now that he had left them. How gently and how gradually he led them into an assurance of his loving concern for them. He began in such a gentle way by feeding them and supplying their physical needs first. (Sit and watch the charcoal fire ebb away fulfilling its purpose.)

Colloquy: Jesus, you are always showing the same loving concern for me. As I pause to reflect on the long litany of your countless gifts I am overwhelmed with your goodness. It is impossible to thank you for each one, but let my heart just sing your praises and let it be filled with gratitude.

FOURTH REFLECTION

v. 15 " 'Simon, son of John, do you love me more than these?' 'Yes, Lord,' he said, 'you know that I love you.' At which Jesus said, 'Feed my lambs.' "

Peter had denied Jesus three times. Sorrow overwhelmed his heart to such an extent that he was not able to express in words the deep feelings of regret and contrition. Jesus did not exact any sort of apology or confession of guilt. All he wanted was the assurance of Peter's love. Jesus did not need this confirmation, but Peter did. He needed to know that Jesus was concerned about whether or not Peter loved him. Peter needed to express his love in order to be healed of the sense of guilt. Jesus expressed his loving acceptance of Peter by commissioning him to "Feed my lambs." This gave Peter the assurance that all was forgiven and that Jesus had confidence in him. (Listen to Jesus ask you: "Do you love me?")

Colloquy: Jesus, you ask me to express my love also. I need to hear myself verbalizing my love in order to strengthen my love within myself. Jesus, please continue to ask for my love, so that I may grow in that love. Thank you for loving me.

FIFTH REFLECTION

v. 16 "A second time he put his question, 'Simon, son of John, do you love me'?"

Jesus knew that Peter regretted deeply his denial of him at the very moment when Jesus needed him most. The hurt was deep-seated. Jesus wanted a total healing for Peter. This is why he asked him the second time if he loved him. Peter needed a second time to hear himself express his love for Jesus so that more healing could take place and more of the sense of guilt be washed away. It was not a question of Jesus doubting Peter's sincerity—after all, Jesus could read hearts—but Peter needed to know that Jesus was vitally concerned about him and that he loved Peter deeply. Again Jesus gives Peter that reassurance of his love: "Tend my sheep." (Listen to yourself repeating your love for Jesus.)

Colloquy: Jesus, you show the same loving concern for me that you showed Peter. Sometimes I do not understand your ways, because my heart is not in tune with yours. Continue to fill my heart with your love. Let it overflow to wash away any sense of guilt. Let me hear you say that you love me regardless of what I have done.

SIXTH REFLECTION

v. 17 "A third time, Jesus asked him, 'Simon, son of John, do you love me?' . . . 'Lord, you know everything. You know well that I love you.' . . . 'Feed my sheep.' "

For a moment Simon thought that Jesus was doubting his honesty and sincerity by asking him the third time for an expression of his love. After a brief reflection Peter realized that Jesus wanted him to recognize his own weakness, his own inability to love unless he depended on Jesus. How humbly he turned to Jesus and said in effect: Lord, you know I want to love you. You know I am trying to love you, but I learned my lesson that I cannot do it of myself. I must depend solely on your gift to be able to love you. Do we see ourselves in Peter? So often we launch out with the intention of doing great things for God and for others only to discover that we have failed time and time again. Perhaps we have depended too much on ourselves. Jesus needs to ask us if we love him, and if we do, then we will let him help us. In his great love for us, he wants to be a part of our lives. If we truly love him, we will let him. (Listen to Jesus ask you again: "Do you really love?")

Colloquy: Lord Jesus, thank you for giving me an example in St. Peter. I too boast of all that I am going to do for you, only to fail miserably because I did not come to you with genuine poverty of spirit. I come now to beg you to mold, shape, form and transform my heart so that you can fill it with your love and it may beat in unison with your Sacred Heart.

SEVENTH REFLECTION

vv. 18-19 "I tell you solemnly . . . another will tie you fast and carry you off against your will . . . . Follow me."

Jesus was leading Peter into the real test of his love. Jesus prepared Peter for the price he would have to pay for his total commitment in love to Jesus. If Peter really loved Jesus, and he did, then he would be asked for that total act of love: martyrdom. If Peter was going to be loyal to Jesus and faithful in his commission to feed the sheep then he, like his Master, would be misunderstood, misjudged and eventually put to death. Jesus loved us so completely that he could give nothing less than himself. If we are to be his true followers, then we must die to self every day. We may not be led off to execution or martyrdom, but we will be asked to suffer the hundred and one pinpricks of every day. This too can be a martyrdom. Jesus bade Peter and he bids us: "Follow me." (Ask yourself how far are you willing to follow Jesus.)

Colloquy: Jesus, you told us that every disciple must be willing to take up his cross daily and follow you. I know that I cannot fulfill my mission in life unless I take you literally. My human nature rebels at times against the cross. I need your help and your reassurance. You did promise that your grace would be sufficient for me, and I am counting on it.

Some scriptural references to continue your prayer:

I Peter 1:3-10   "Although you have never seen him, you love him. . . ."

I John 1:1-3   "We have seen and bear witness to it . . . ."

John 1:35-51   "Come and see. . . ."
Luke 9:23-27   "Whoever wishes to be my
                  follower must deny his very
                  self. . . ."
Mark 10:17-31   "Go and sell what you have. . . .
                  come and follow me."

29 Pentecost

"All Were Filled With The Holy Spirit"
Acts: Chapters 1 & 2

Pope John XXIII asked us to pray for the outpouring of the Holy Spirit with his signs and wonders in a New Pentecost as it were. We prayed and the Holy Spirit responded far more generously than we dared to anticipate. Since then we have become much more aware of the presence and power of the Holy Spirit in our lives. Jesus knew that it would be difficult for the apostles to grasp the role of the Holy Spirit in their lives and in the early Church; therefore, he instructed them to return to the Upper Room and there spend their time in prayer. They did, and as a result they became open and receptive to the release of the Holy Spirit within them. We know the signs and wonders which followed to this very day. Like the apostles we need to spend time in prayer, listening with our whole being to what the Holy Spirit is saying to us.

FIRST REFLECTION

Acts 1:8 "You will receive power when the Holy Spirit comes down on you; then you are to be my witnesses in Jerusalem, throughout Judea and Samaria, yes, even to the ends of the earth."

In his discourse at the Last Supper Jesus promised us that he would not leave us orphans. He also promised us that he would send us another Paraclete. He went on to tell us what the Holy Spirit would do for us. When Jesus was about to ascend into heaven, he reiterated that promise. "You will receive power when the Holy Spirit comes down on you." We are the temples of the Holy Spirit. He is living within us. He is empowering us with his gifts. Only by his power are we able to produce those special fruits of the Spirit. What a privilege is ours! What dignity is ours! Jesus tells us that "he (the Spirit) will bear witness on my behalf. You must bear witness as well" (*John 15:26*). Our witness consists primarily in reflecting the love, peace and joy which the Spirit produces within us. Our witness will be fruitful because of what we are rather than because of the things we do. (Rest in the Spirit. Let him fill you.)

Colloquy: Come Holy Spirit, fill me with your presence and your power. Help me to empty myself so that you can become more operative within me. Keep me ever aware of your abiding presence so that I can better relate to you. Release your power within me so that I may become a faithful witness.

SECOND REFLECTION

vv. 12-14 "They went to the upstairs room . . . . Together they devoted themselves to constant prayer."

Jesus had instructed his apostles: "Remain here in the city until you are clothed with power from on high" (*Luke 24:49*). The apostles began to understand gradually the significance of the events transpiring in such rapid succession. They were getting new insights into the mission to which Jesus had called them. They prepared themselves for the coming of the Holy Spirit by spending these next ten days in prayer. They wanted to be receptive to what the Spirit was going to do for them. They needed to ponder all that was happening. Mary, the Mother of Jesus, was with them in that upstairs room. How Mary must have poured out her heart in prayer! She understood already the power of the Holy Spirit in her. She knew what a transformation he could work in the apostles. Mary was already regarded as the "Mother of the Church" and she prayed for the success of the infant Church in these critical days. (Be present in the Upper Room. Pray with the apostles and Mary.)

Colloquy: Jesus, thank you for encouraging the apostles to pray in the Cenacle. What a valuable lesson for me! I need to spend much more time in prayer so that I can be an empty vessel for the Spirit to fill with his purifying love and his transforming power. Teach me the necessity of prayer and grant me the desire to want to pray always.

THIRD REFLECTION

v. 2 (Acts 2) "Suddenly from up in the sky there came a noise like a strong, driving wind which was heard all through the house where they were seated."

The Blessed Trinity is a deep mystery. We cannot fathom it. We can have some concept of the Father and the Son, but we cannot visualize the Holy Spirit. Scripture uses all sorts of symbols to depict the Holy Spirit. Jesus said we can know a tree by its fruits. We can know the Holy Spirit by what he accomplishes in us. The mighty wind symbolizes his power. His work is to purify and sanctify us. He pours out his many gifts upon us so that we can fulfill our mission of building up the body of Christ, the Church. He produces in us his fruit, especially love of which all the other fruits are component parts. Since he is Spirit, his presence had to be manifested in this physical way—noise and wind—so that the apostles could be aware of what was happening to them. (Rest in the Spirit and let him fill you with his love.)

Colloquy: "Come Holy Spirit, I need you. Come Holy Spirit, I pray. Come with your strength and power. Come in your gentle way."

FOURTH REFLECTION

v. 3 "Tongues as of fire appeared, which parted and came to rest on each of them."

There is much mystery about the Holy Spirit, but we do know that he is the Spirit of love, the very source of love. This symbolism is apparent in the descent of the Holy Spirit on this first Pentecost. He came in the form of fiery tongues. Fire symbolized his burning love for us. He came and settled upon each of them in order to fill them with his love so that they in turn might become channels of love to others. The disciples had to be filled with love in order to make their total commitment to the apostolate to which Jesus had called them. Secondly, in order to be effective in their mission, they had to radiate the love, peace and joy of the Spirit. The Spirit makes us his temples so that he can fill us with his love. His love is limitless. It depends solely on our capacity to receive it. (Experience the love of God within you.)

Colloquy: Come Holy Spirit, inflame my heart with the fire of your love. Let me be an open channel of your love to everyone I meet. Teach me to love my neighbor as you would have me. That is an apostolate all of its own. Grant me that grace.

FIFTH REFLECTION

v. 4 "All were filled with the Holy Spirit. They began to express themselves in foreign tongues and make bold proclamations as the Spirit prompted them."

A great change suddenly came over the apostles. They had deserted Jesus in the Garden of Gethsemane.

With the exception of John, they had abandoned him on Calvary. Now they were concealed here in the Cenacle with all the doors securely locked, frightened of their fate if the enemies of Jesus discovered them. After the coming of the Holy Spirit they stepped out with great courage and boldness. They were eager and anxious to proclaim the good news to whomever would listen. Fear was gone. Their timidity evaporated. Furthermore, these unlettered men now spoke eloquently and intelligently to the astonishment of everyone. All their hearers were amazed. This obviously was the work of the Spirit. That same Spirit is at work in us if we continue to be receptive to his divine influence. (Rest in his presence and let his strength permeate you.)

Colloquy: Lord Jesus, you have called me to be your follower. How timid and self-conscious I am. I am too fearful to speak out and proclaim your Word. Send your Holy Spirit to fill me with his gifts of wisdom, knowledge and understanding so that I may be your witness.

SIXTH REFLECTION

v. 32-33 "This is the Jesus God has raised up, and we are his witnesses. Exalted at God's right hand, he first received the promised Holy Spirit from the Father, then poured this Spirit out on us."

Jesus had promised to send us the Holy Spirit. On Pentecost he fulfilled that promise with the outpouring of the Spirit as was so evident by the visible signs of noise, wind and tongues as of fire. Jesus also told us what the Spirit would do for us when he did come. He would be with us always. He will instruct us in everything and remind us of all that Jesus told us. He will guide us to all truth (*John 14 & 16*). This is precisely what the Spirit did in the apostles on the first Pentecost, especially in St. Peter as he delivered this lengthy discourse. The Spirit will also teach us by showing us how we must live according to the Way which Jesus taught us. He will help us to be witnesses of Jesus. When the Spirit does so, we will stand in awe and reverence because we will recognize that it is not ourselves who are speaking and witnessing. We, like the apostles, will be able to declare what the Spirit has put into our hearts. (Pause and reflect on what the Spirit is effecting in you at this moment.)

Colloquy: Jesus, you told me so plainly that apart from you I can do nothing. You also promised that with the power and presence of your Spirit in me, I could do all things. Help me to empty myself, to come with genuine poverty of spirit, so that you can pour out your Spirit on me.

SEVENTH REFLECTION

v. 38 "You must reform and be baptized, each one of you, in the name of Jesus Christ, that your sins may be forgiven; then you will receive the gift of the Holy Spirit."

In his first discourse, Peter spoke out boldly and honestly, setting forth what God requires of us in order to be filled with his Spirit and to walk daily in his presence. John the Baptist had repeatedly insisted on the necessity of repentance. "He went about the entire region of the Jordan proclaiming a baptism of repentance which led to the forgiveness of sins" (*Luke 3:3*). Jesus likewise insisted on a complete change of heart. We need a constant conversion. Our human nature becomes so engrossed with the mundane, so absorbed with the temporalities which daily engulf us, that we soon lose our focus on our loving Father. We need constantly to refocus our attention Godward, to adjust our course so that God will become our number-one priority in life. This is the work the Holy Spirit effects in us if we will permit him to work freely. (In your prayer, look Godward.)

Colloquy: O Holy Spirit, dwelling within me, release your power and your love so that my course may ever be directed toward you. Grant me a secure sense of direction. Rescue me when I turn off on some tangent. Enlighten me, guide me, lead me always closer to Jesus. There are a number of other Pentecosts which you may wish to ponder in your prayer:

John 20:22	"Receive the Holy Spirit."
Acts 10:44-48	"The Holy Spirit descended upon all who were listening to Peter's message."
Acts 19:1-7	"As Paul laid his hands on them, the Holy Spirit came down on them. . . ."

In his Last Discourse in the Upper Room, Jesus also told us what the Holy Spirit would do for us:

John 14:16-18	". . . he remains with you and will be within you."
John 14:25-26	"The Holy Spirit . . . will instruct you in everything. . . ."
John 15: 26-27	". . . he will bear witness on my behalf."
John 16:5-14	". . . he will guide you to all truth."

30 Living With the Risen Jesus

"Who Will Separate Us From The Love Of Christ?"
Romans 8:1-39

We value a close friendship. A friend is a person who understands us and can affirm and encourage us when we need it. We can openly and honestly share all our joys and sorrows with a true friend. A friend gives us the assurance that someone really cares about us. Jesus is such a friend and more. There is no other friendship which can be compared with our relationship with Jesus. He not only lives with us, but within us. After his resurrection he was able to share his divine life with us so that he becomes a very part of our being. He inspires our thoughts; he strengthens us; he fills us with his love. Truly we are living with the Risen Jesus. This truth makes our journey through life more delightful and more fruitful.

FIRST REFLECTION

vv. 1-13 ". . . . the Spirit of God dwells in you . . . will bring your mortal bodies to life through his Spirit dwelling in you."

The Holy Spirit is the full gift of Jesus dwelling within us. They are inseparable. We are the temples of the Holy Spirit. "Are you not aware that you are the temple of God, and that the Spirit of God dwells in you?" *(I Cor. 3:16)*. "You are the temple of the living God" *(II Cor. 6:16)*. This brings us new life. Jesus is

·dwelling in us through the power of his Spirit. We are never alone. Jesus knows our joys and sorrows, our hopes and ambitions, our successes and our failures, our hurts and our happiness. His divine life is permeating our whole being. What dignity is ours! We never have to accomplish anything alone. Jesus through the power of his Spirit is strengthening and supporting us. He is guiding and encouraging us. There is no cause for fear, no reason for loneliness. What a privilege to be a Christian! (Relax and let the divine life surge through your whole being.)

Colloquy: Lord Jesus, thank you for the magnificent gift of your Holy Spirit. There is such a mystery about his presence that I cannot comprehend the extraordinary privilege which is mine. Let me relate in everything to your divine presence within me.

SECOND REFLECTION

vv. 14-15 "All who are led by the Spirit of God are sons of God."

Our loving Father has invited us to become members of his family. He adopted us by sharing his divine life with us. All this took place through the sacramental rite of Baptism. God is not a remote deity, far away in his heaven, leaving us to struggle through life's maze of problems. No, he is our loving Father who lives with us. He loves us as his children so that we may call him our "Abba." He is our "Daddy." This is not merely a pious expression; it speaks of the close, intimate, loving relationship which the Father has with his children. He loves us. How often he tries to tell us in his Word that he loves us with a creative love, with a concerned and caring love, with a forgiving, healing love, with an enduring love. If our Father loves us so totally what else really matters? Nothing. (Bask in the sunshine of your Abba's love.)

200

Colloquy: Lord Jesus, by your passion, death and resurrection, you obtained this great privilege and dignity for me. Your Father is my Father and you come to dwell within me through the power of your Holy Spirit. Grant me the grace always to respond to this great dignity and to reflect your indwelling in all that I do and say.

THIRD REFLECTION

vv. 16-17 "If we are children, we are heirs as well: heirs of God, heirs with Christ. . . ."

By virtue of our Baptism we are children of the Father and heirs of God. This means that all that our loving Father has will be ours. His greatest gift to us is the gift of himself.

Heaven is our total union with our Father. It is a union of perfect love. We are also "heirs with Christ" which means that Jesus is our brother. He was incarnated into our world, he took on our human flesh so that he could become one of us. Thus united with us, he could lead us through our death to be united with our Father in heaven. Death is only the doorway through which our brother Jesus leads us to the Father. Jesus conquered death so that we could become heirs for all eternity. (Rest with Jesus your brother.)

Colloquy: Jesus, my brother, because of your great love for me I can cry out with Paul: "O death, where is your victory? O death, where is your sting?" By your own sacrificial death on the cross, "death is swallowed up in victory." This outpouring of your love just overwhelms me. Continue to love me and remove from me every fear of death. Keep reminding me that you are my brother who has gone to prepare a place for me and that you are even now waiting to shower your divine life upon me in all its fullness.

FOURTH REFLECTION

vv. 18-25 "We ourselves, although we have the Spirit as first fruits, groan inwardly while we await the redemption of our bodies."

By means of the whole paschal mystery of the passion, death and resurrection of Jesus, we share in his divine life. He is dwelling within us, but only in a limited way. We do not have the capacity to receive his divine life in all its fullness. For this reason we are struggling with the vicissitudes of life. Our way is often a *via dolorsa* even though it may be sprinkled with joy, peace and happiness at every step. Amid our earthly struggle there is hope because we are moving ever onward toward our own resurrection. We have received the Spirit and he is a guarantee of our way leading to eternal union with our Father. As Paul puts it: "I consider the sufferings of the present to be as nothing compared with the glory to be revealed in us" *(Rom. 8:18)*. What hope this brings us! What joy in knowing God's love for us! What a destiny awaits us! (Let your heart rejoice in the expectation of God's loving plan for you.)

Colloquy: Jesus, you were able to endure your cruel passion and death because you understood what fruits would accrue to me because of it. As I continue my pilgrimage through life be at my side to remind me of the joy which awaits me. Fill me with "patient endurance.' "

Let me rejoice in the great love you shower upon me.

FIFTH REFLECTION

vv. 26-27 "The Spirit too helps us in our weakness, for we do not know how to pray as we ought. . . ."

Prayer is simply my relationship to God. Prayer is a gift from God. The Holy Spirit instills in us the desire to want to pray. He creates in our hearts a desire and hunger to be along with God our Father. As we reach out to God in prayer our own Spirit unites itself with the Holy Spirit. When our spirit is in tune with His Spirit there is no need for words, not even for any brilliant thoughts. We are happy just to rest in the security of his presence and his love. Our hearts seems to beat in unison with him. Such prayer is a gift from God. He asks only for the gift of ourselves when we are silent, alone with him and listening with our whole being. At the very core of silence we will find God. (Let the Spirit get in touch with your spirit.)

Colloquy: Jesus, one day your disciples gathered around you when they saw you in prayer and they asked: "Lord, teach us to pray." Pour your Holy Spirit upon me that he may lead me into a deep, rich prayerful union with you. "No one can say: 'Jesus is Lord' except in the Holy Spirit." Grant me that gift. I want you to be my Lord.

SIXTH REFLECTION

vv. 28-34 "Those he predestined he likewise called; those he called he also justified; and those he justified he in turn glorified."

Our loving Father called each one of us into existence at this particular time in salvation history. He sent his Son to justify us by his redeeming love. He poured his Spirit upon us that we may be glorified. What else could he have done for us and he has not yet done it? Of all the myriad persons living why should God have predestined me? There is only one answer and that is his infinite love for me. An awareness of this kind of love causes everything else in life to fade into the shadows. As Paul says: "If God is for us, who can be against us?" If Jesus is living in us through the power of his Holy Spirit what else really matters? Very little. We have an added assurance that this predestination is ours because of Jesus "who is at the right hand of God and who intercedes for us." (Let this mystery settle into your whole being.)

Colloquy: Jesus you are living with me. You are dwelling within me. I am never alone. How can I fathom this mystery of your love? May its significance sink deep into my heart. May your abiding love become the guiding star in my life.

SEVENTH REFLECTION

vv. 35-39 "Who will separate us from the love of Christ? . . . [who] will be able to separate us from the love of God that comes to us in Christ Jesus, our Lord."

If you are living with the risen Jesus and if his Spirit is living within us, then our whole focus on life changes. The temporalities of every day lose much of their importance. Sin becomes less and less attractive. The desire to be with Jesus and to love him more and more increases within our hearts. God reveals his great love for us so that we will be better enabled to respond to him in love. Love must be the impelling power in our lives. If so, nothing can separate us from the love of God. If my focus is on a distant object which I am eagerly trying to reach then I take no notice of the little things closer to me. They do not captivate my imagination at all. This is one of the reasons why Jesus came into the world not as a guest, but to stay. (Let God's love envelop you.)

Colloquy: O Jesus, in spite of your gracious love for me, I am still a weak, sinful human being. Never let anything separate me from your love. Draw me closer to you with "the bands of your love." To live with the Risen Jesus, we must pause frequently to listen to his Word, to converse with him, to let him remind us of his abiding love. Here are a few suggestions:

John 15: 1-17	"Live on in my love."
I John 5: 1-13	"Who, then, is conqueror of the world?"

Acts 17:28   "In him we live and more and have our being. . . ."

Hebrews 12: 1-13   "Let us keep our eyes fixed on Jesus, who inspires and perfects our faith."

There are many Pauline texts which encourage us to live with the Risen Jesus.

31. Finding God in All Things

*"When You Seek Me With All Your Heart, You Will Find
Me With You."*
John 1: 1-18

To enable you to find God in all things, visualize God
standing at your side and pointing out to you every
phase of his creation, even the most minute aspect of it.
Listen to him as he explains how his providence has
supplied your every possible need at every turn of the
road. As he asks you if there is anything he might have
created for you and didn't, try to answer. When he
inquires what else he might have provided for you and
didn't, again attempt to answer. As we reflect on God's
creative, caring, providing, forgiving, healing, enduring love, we will find him. As he himself says: "When
you look for me, you will find me."

FIRST REFLECTION

v. 1 "In the beginning was the Word; the Word was in
    God's presence, and the Word was God."

In our attempt to find God in all things, we must also
know who Jesus is. In this single verse of Sacred Scripture, we learn that the Word coexisted with the Father
from all eternity: "In the beginning was the Word."
This expression means that Jesus is timeless. Secondly,
the relationship between Jesus and the Father is expressed briefly, but aptly in: "The Word was in God's
presence." Finally, Jesus is identified with God: "And

the Word was God." This short statement prepares us for the ministry which Jesus came to fulfill. Since Jesus is God, then his mission of bringing the good news and his work of redemption is the manifestation of the Holy Trinity's profound love for us. We find God in all his works. (Let all the implications of this statement fill you.)

Colloquy: Lord Jesus, you are truly God. You are the Alpha and the Omega of my whole being. I adore you and worship you. I thank you for your love. I want to love you in return.

SECOND REFLECTION

vv. 3-5 "Through him all things came into being, and apart from him nothing came to be."

Jesus is found in all the works of creation. He is the Creator. "In him everything in heaven and on earth was created . . . all were created through him, and for him" *(Colossians 1:16)*. God created the entire universe for us his creatures. He created the sun, moon and stars. He made the land and sea, the mountains and the valleys. All the fruits of the field are the gift of his creative love. He provides the fresh air we breathe as well as the water we drink. Every heartbeat is a special gift from him. We can find God at our fingertips as we reflect on his creation. There is nothing which he has not created and given into the custody of man for his use and enjoyment. Yes, God is present to us in his creation at every moment of the day. (Try to discover something which is not really his gift.)

Colloquy: Father, I stand in admiration at the totality of your gifts to me. There is nothing about my whole body which you have not created perfectly. Your creation surrounds me on every side. I praise you and I thank you for the love which prompted you to provide every detail of my life.

THIRD REFLECTION

v. 10 "He was in the world, and through him the world was made, yet the world did not know who he was."

God is so present in all of his creation. The glories of an evening sunset, the beauty of a rose, the smile of a child—all speak to us about a God of love. Jesus came into the world to announce the good news that our God is a God of love. Even though he healed, calmed the sea, raised the dead, "the world did not know who he was." Their faith was not strong enough to recognize the divine presence and power in his works. Jesus appealed to us in these words: "Believe me that I am in the Father and the Father is in me, or else, believe because of the works I do" *(John 14:11)*. As we strive to find God in all things, let us pause to observe the works of God all around us. Listen to Jesus as he points out the love which the Father has for us in giving us all that we enjoy. (Gaze in wonder at God's works.)

Colloquy: Jesus, you are so present in my life, yet how often I am too busy to recognize or acknowledge you and your marvelous works. Teach me to pause, to ponder in prayer, and then to praise you for the wonders of your love.

FOURTH REFLECTION

vv. 11-12 "To his own he came, yet his own did not accept him. Any who did accept him he empowered to become children of God."

It is not surprising that the world did not accept Jesus, nor recognize him in all his works. How much more tragic it is that his own did not accept him. They could see all the signs and wonders wrought by his creative, caring love, but they closed their hearts to him. Their minds refused to acknowledge that he could be the "Promised" of the ages. He offered them the gift of faith, but they ignored him. On the other hand, those who did accept him "he empowered to become the children of God." He shared his divine life with us and thus adopted us as his children. He gave us the faith to recognize and accept him. He opened our eyes that we might find him in all the splendors of his creation around us. What more could he have done? (Thank Jesus for the gift of your faith.)

Colloquy: Lord Jesus, how you have blessed and gifted me with the faith to recognize and accept you as my Lord and my God. More than that you adopted me as your child. Help me to live up to the dignity which you gave me. May I never embarrass you by my life.

FIFTH REFLECTION

v. 14 "The Word became flesh and made his dwelling among us, and we have seen his glory; the glory of an only Son coming from the Father, filled with enduring love."

Jesus came into the world that we may know more about God, our Father. He came also that we might recognize him. He did all this to prove to us how much the Father loves us and how much Jesus himself loves us. John says: "Yes, God so loved the world that he gave his only Son" *(John 3:16).* Jesus became incarnated into the world to make "his dwelling among us." In the Sinai desert God made his dwelling among his people. It was only a representation and a reminder of his presence. Jesus came in the flesh to remain with us in his resurrected life. His dwelling was permanent. His dwelling is not only with us, but he is living within us. The glory of Jesus is the work of his redemption within each of us. He has done all this for us because he came "from the Father, filled with enduring love." That love will never change regardless of what we may do. And the Father reminds us: "With age-old love I have loved you" *(Jeremiah 31:3).* This is the God we want to know better each day. (Rest in his presence and let Jesus love you.)

Colloquy: Thank you, Father, for loving me so much

that you gave us your only Son, Jesus. Thank you, Jesus, for loving me with an enduring love. Help me to find you always in the love which you are showering upon me. I want to love you in return.

SIXTH REFLECTION

v. 16 "Of his fullness we have all had a share—love following upon love."

God's love for us is absolutely infinite. It cannot be any greater. Jesus came into the world that he might share this love with us. God is love. Since he is love and since he shares his love with us, he is sharing himself, his divine life. Jesus shares his love with us by permitting love to follow love. In his love he shares his gifts with us. He never fails us. Each breath is a gift from God. One breath following upon another is certainly one love following upon love. The Father continues to bless us by his endless bestowal of gifts upon us through Jesus. Jesus asks us to respond in love so that our lives may become "love following upon love."

SEVENTH REFLECTION

v. 18 "No one has ever seen God. It is God the only Son, ever at the Father's side, who has revealed him."

The purpose of this contemplation is to find God in all things. We can know the Father only through the Son. Jesus told us: "No one comes to the Father but through me" (John 14:6). And again Jesus said: "No one knows the Son but the Father, and no one knows the Father but the Son—and anyone to whom the Son wishes to reveal him" (Matthew 11:27). Jesus came into the world to reveal the Father to us. Jesus showed us in reality and in the concrete that his Father is a God who loves us. Jesus manifested his great love for us by all that he did for us: healing, comforting, teaching, and above all by laying down his life for us. He was saying in effect: "This is how much your Father loves you too

for the Father and I are one." (Be still and let Jesus
reveal the Father to you.)

Colloquy: Jesus, let me settle down so that you can
reveal the Father to me. Let me experience his love for
me. Let me rejoice in the awareness that the Father
loves me and that you love me to such an extent that
you laid down your life for me. Thank you, Jesus. The
following are a few scriptural passages which will help
you find God in all things:

Colossians 1: 15-20   "He is the image of the invisible
                        God. . . ."
Ephesians 1: 3 to 2:10 "Praised be the God and Father
                        of our Lord Jesus Christ. . . ."

There are many psalms praising God's loving kindness. Here are only a few suggestions:
Psalms 8 - 103 - 104 - 139 - 148.

LINGER WITH ME
Moments Aside with Jesus   2.95

Rev. Msgr. David E. Rosage. God is calling us to a listening
posture in prayer in the desire to experience him at the very core
of our being. Monsignor Rosage helps us to "come by ourselves
apart" and listen to what Jesus is telling us in Scripture.

PRAYING WITH SCRIPTURE IN THE HOLY LAND:
Daily Meditations With the Risen Jesus   2.50

Msgr. David E. Rosage. Herein is offered a daily meeting with the
Risen Jesus in those Holy Places which He sanctified by His human
presence. Three hundred and sixty-five scripture texts are selected
and blended with the pilgrimage experiences of the author, a retreat
master, and well-known writer on prayer.

DISCOVERING PATHWAYS TO PRAYER   1.95

Msgr. David E. Rosage. Following Jesus was never meant to be dull,
or worse, just duty-filled. Those who would aspire to a life of prayer
and those who have already begun, will find this book amazingly
thorough in its scripture-punctuated approach.

*"A simple but profound book which explains the many ways and
forms of prayer by which the person hungering for closer union
with God may find him."* **Emmnauel Spillane, O.C.S.O., Abbot, Our
Lady of the Holy Trinity Abbey, Huntsville, Utah.**

REASONS FOR REJOICING
Experiences in Christian Hope   1.75

Rev. Kenneth J. Zanca. The author asks: "Do we really or rarely
have a sense of excitement, mystery, and wonder in the presence of
God?" His book offers a path to rejuvenation in Christian faith,
hope, and love. It deals with prayer, forgiveness, worship and other
religious experiences in a learned and penetrating, yet simple, non-
technical manner. **Religion Teachers' Journal.**

*"It is a refreshing Christian approach to the Good News, always
emphasizing the love and mercy of God in our lives, and our response to that love in Christian hope."* **Brother Patrick Hart, Secre-
tary to the late Thomas Merton.**

MARY:
Pathway to Fruitfulness

1.95

John Randall, STD., Helen P. Hawkinson, Sharyn Malloy. Mary is shown to be an exemplar of fruitful Christian living in her role as model relative, suffering servant and seat of wisdom. Her growing role as mediator between Catholics and Protestants is also highlighted.

FORMED BY HIS WORD:
Scriptural Patterns of Prayer

1.95

Rev. Malcolm Cornwell, C.P. Commentary on St. Luke; a set of teachings suitable for people seeking guidance in prayer.

JONAH:
Spirituality of a Runaway Prophet

1.75

Roman Ginn, o.c.s.o. While acquiring a new appreciation for this very human prophet, we come to see that his story is really our own. It reveals a God whose love is unwavering yet demanding, for if we are to experience the freedom of mature Christians, we must enter the darkness of the tomb with Christ, as Jonah did, in order to rise to new life.

POOR IN SPIRIT:
Awaiting All From God

1.75

Cardinal Garrone. Not a biography of the Mother Teresa of her age, this spiritual account of Jeanne Jugan's complete and joyful abandonment to God leads us to a vibrant understanding of spiritual and material poverty.

DESERT SILENCE:
A Way of Prayer for an Unquiet Age

1.75

Rev. Alan J. Placa. The pioneering efforts of the men and women of the early church who went out into the desert to find union with the Lord has relevance for those of us today who are seeking the pure uncluttered desert place within to have it filled with the loving silence of God's presence.

Order from your bookstore or
LIVING FLAME PRESS, Locust Valley, N.Y. 11560

PROMPTED BY THE SPIRIT

2.50

Rev. Paul Sauvé. A handbook by a Catholic Charismatic Renewal national leader for all seriously concerned about the future of the renewal and interested in finding answers to some of the problems that have surfaced in small or large prayer groups. It is a call to all Christians to find answers with the help of a wise Church tradition as transmitted by her ordained ministers. The author has also written *Petals of Prayer/Creative Ways to Pray.*

THE BOOK OF REVELATION:
What Does It Really Say?

1.75

Rev. John Randall, S.T.D. The most discussed book of the Bible today is examined by a scripture expert in relation to much that has been published on the Truth. A simply written and revealing presentation.

. . . AND I WILL FILL THIS HOUSE WITH GLORY:
Renewal Within a Suburban Parish

1.50

Rev. James A. Brassil. This book helps answer the questions: What is the Charismatic Renewal doing for the Church as a whole? and What is the prayer group doing for the parish? With a vibrant prayer life and a profound devotion to the Eucharist, this Long Island prayer group has successfully endured the growing pains inherent to the spiritual life, the fruit of which is offered to the reader.

CONTEMPLATIVE PRAYER:
Problems and An Approach for the Ordinary Christian 1.75

Rev. Alan J. Placa. This inspiring book covers much ground: the struggle of prayer, growth in familiarity with the Lord and the sharing process. In addition, he clearly outlines a method of contemplative prayer for small groups based on the belief that private communion with God is essential to, and must precede, shared prayer. The last chapter provides model prayers, taken from our Western heritage, for the enrichment of private prayer experience.

**Order from your bookstore or
LIVING FLAME PRESS, Locust Valley, N.Y. 11560**

THE ONE WHO LISTENS:
A Book of Prayer

2.25

Rev. Michael Hollings and Etta Gullick. Here the Spirit speaks through men and women of the past (St. John of the Cross, Thomas More, Dietrich Bonhoeffer), and present (Michel Quoist, Mother Teresa, Malcolm Boyd). There are also prayers from men of other faiths such as Muhammed and Tagore. God meets us where we are and since men share in sorrow, joy and anxiety, *their* prayers are *our* prayers. This is a book that will be outworn, perhaps, but never outgrown.

ENFOLDED BY CHRIST:
An Encouragement to Pray

1.95

Rev. Michael Hollings. This book helps us toward giving our lives to God in prayer yet at the same time remaining totally available to our fellowman — a difficult but possible feat. Father's sharing of his own difficulties and his personal approach convince us that "if he can do it, we can." We find in the author a true spiritual guardian and friend.

SOURCE OF LIFE:
The Eucharist and Christian Living

1.50

Rev. Rene Voillaume. A powerful testimony to the vital part the Eucharist plays in the life of a Christian. It is a product of a man for whom Christ in the Eucharist is nothing less than all.

SEEKING PURITY OF HEART:
The Gift of Ourselves to God

illus. 1.50

Joseph Breault. For those of us who feel that we do not live up to God's calling, that we have sin of whatever shade within our hearts. This book shows how we can begin a journey which will lead from our personal darkness to wholeness in Christ's light — a purity of heart. Clear, practical help is given us in the constant struggle to free ourselves from the deceptions that sin has planted along all avenues of our lives.

Order from your bookstore or
LIVING FLAME PRESS, Locust Valley, N.Y. 11560

Books by Venard Polusney, O. Carm.

UNION WITH THE LORD IN PRAYER
Beyond Meditation To Affective Prayer Aspiration And Contemplation
1.00

"A magnificent piece of work. It touches on all the essential points of Contemplative Prayer. Yet it brings such a sublime subject down to the level of comprehension of the 'man in the street,' and in such an encouraging way."
Abbott James Fox, O.C.S.O. (former superior of Thomas Merton at the Abbey of Gethsemani)

ATTAINING SPIRITUAL MATURITY FOR CONTEMPLATION (According to St. John of the Cross)
1.00

"I heartily recommend this work with great joy that at last the sublime teachings of St. John of the Cross have been brought down to the understanding of the ordinary Christian without at the same time watering them down. For all (particularly for charismatic Christians) hungry for greater contemplation."
Rev. George A. Maloney, S.J., Editor of Diakonia, Professor of Patristics and Spirituality, Fordham University.

THE PRAYER OF LOVE ... THE ART OF ASPIRATION
1.95

"It is the best book I have read which evokes the simple and loving response to remain in love with the Lover. To read it meditatively, to imbibe its message of love, is to have it touch your life and become part of what you are."
Mother Dorothy Guilbuilt, O. Carm., Superior General, Lacombe, La.

Order from your bookstore or
LIVING FLAME PRESS, Locust Valley, N.Y. 11560

LIVING FLAME PRESS
BOX 74, LOCUST VALLEY, N.Y. 11560

Quantity

_____ **Linger with Me — 2.95**

_____ **Mary: Pathway to Fruitfulness — 1.95**

_____ **The Judas Within — 1.95**

_____ **Formed by His Word — 1.95**

_____ **Jonah — 1.75**

_____ **Poor in Spirit — 1.75**

_____ **Desert Silence — 1.75**

_____ **Praying With Scripture in the Holy Land — 2.50**

_____ **Discovering Pathways to Prayer — 1.95**

_____ **Reasons for Rejoicing — 1.75**

_____ **Contemplative Prayer — 1.75**

_____ **The One Who Listens — 2.25**

_____ **Enfolded by Christ — 1.95**

_____ **Source of Life — 1.50**

_____ **Seeking Purity of Heart — 1.50**

_____ **Prompted by the Spirit — 2.50**

_____ **The Book of Revelation — 1.75**

_____ **And I Will Fill This House With Glory — 1.50**

_____ **Union With the Lord in Prayer — 1.00**

_____ **Attaining Spiritual Maturity — 1.00**

_____ **The Prayer of Love — 1.95**

QUANTITY ORDER: DISCOUNT RATES

For convents, prayer groups, etc.: $10 to $25 = 10%;
$26 to $50 = 15%; over $50 = 20%. Booksellers: 40%, 30 days net.

NAME _____

ADDRESS _____

CITY_____ STATE_____ ZIP_____

☐ *Payment enclosed. Kindly include $.50 postage and handling on
order up to $5.00. Above that, include 10% of total up to $20.
Then 7% of total. Thank you.*